Travelling at the Speed of Mind

Travelling at the Speed of Mind

Ngakma Nor'dzin

Aro Books WORLDWIDE

2023

Aro Books WORLDWIDE,

PO Box 111, 5 Court Close,
Cardiff, Wales, CF14 1JR

© 2023 by Ngakma Nor'dzin

All rights reserved. No part of this book may be reproduced in any form or by any means electronic or mechanical, including photocopying, recording, or by any information storage and retrieval system, without permission in writing from the publisher.

Book design, typography and illustrations by Ngakma Nor'dzin.
Thangka painted by the Zorig Thangka Painters' Cooperative, Kathmandu, Nepal.

First Edition 2023

ISBN: 978-1-898185-35-2 (paperback)
ISBN: 978-1-898185-38-3 (ePub)

For further information about Aro Books WORLDWIDE please see http://aro-books-worldwide.org/

To obtain copies of all our publications please visit https://www.lulu.com/spotlight/arobooksworldwide

Contents

Acknowledgments	viii
Foreword	ix
Chapter 1 The Wheel of Life	1
Chapter 2 Yama Lord of Death	17
Chapter 3 The Blank Canvas	31
Chapter 4 Links of Causation	41
Chapter 5 The Six Realms	75
Chapter 6 Going Up or Going Down	109
Chapter 7 The Central Hub	121
Glossary	133

Acknowledgements

'Results come from their own specific conditions. Whether tathagatas appear or not, this true nature of things will remain. It is the true nature; the constancy of Dharma; the immutability of Dharma, consistent with dependent arising, suchness, unmistaken suchness, unchanging suchness, actuality, and truth; unmistaken; and unerring.'
Sutra of the Rice Seedling—stanza 1.9—84000: Translating the Words of the Buddha

My daily Buddhist practice, and knowledge of the teachings is the fruit of the guidance and inspiration of my root Lamas, Ngak'chang Rinpoche and Khandro Déchen. I am eternally grateful for their patience and support.

A teacher arises in response to those who decide to become students. The text has been clarified and developed through the comments and questions of our students. I thank them for their joyful involvement in this process.

One of my greatest teachers is my sang-yab, Ngakpa 'ö-Dzin Tridral – a kind and gentle man. He is quiet when I need to concentrate on writing. He is my researcher when I need help finding a term or a translation. He is my editor when we check the text and find that a sentence is clumsy or unclear. He is my friend at all times, and words are insufficient to express my appreciation of him. It is a wonderful thing to experience the power and strength of sharing our lives in love, practice and everyday contentment.

Foreword

The Wheel of Life is an image that illustrates samsara – cyclic existence. Buddhism teaches that all beings are trapped in a cycle of seeking happiness and satisfaction, only to experience dissatisfaction. The Wheel of Life examines the processes of cyclic existence: the causes which create the cycle, and the effects of being trapped in the cycle. Spiritual practice, and taking full advantage of a Precious Human rebirth, are regarded as the method of escaping cyclic existence.

Rather than footnotes, there is a comprehensive glossary at the end of the book of terms used in the text. The book is presented as a conversation between myself, Ngakpa 'ö-Dzin, and a student, which takes place over the course of a weekend visit. The student, Pema Dorje, represents all our students, and their questions about the Wheel of Life.

Ngakma Nor'dzin,
Cardiff, Wales
December 2022

The Wheel of Life

1 – The Wheel of Life

In a room in suburban Cardiff, a large thangka hangs on a wall. It is an unusual room for South Wales – but traditional in terms of Himalayan Buddhism. The shrine room is decorated according to a particular style of Nyingma Buddhism. The lower part of the walls is a deep red. Then there are two stripes of colour all around the room about as wide as a hand: a green stripe with an orange one above it. The upper part of the walls is a sunshine yellow to the level of the picture rail, which is gold. The wall above the picture rail and the ceiling are a deep deep blue. There are several other thangkas on the walls, but this one is newly arrived.

Pema Dorje (PD): I am happy to see your new thangka of the Wheel of Life. Are you pleased with it?

Ngakma Nor'dzin (NN): Yes. It is beautiful and skilfully painted. I am happy that the thangka painter listened to my requests with regard to colour. So often the colours of thangkas for sale in Kathmandu are rather pastel, and I've seen Yama painted in pink rather than maroon, the colour of dried blood.

PD: The colour of dried blood does feel a bit more wrathful than pink! This image has always been of great interest to you, hasn't it?

NN: Yes, it is a bit of a love affair! I have photographs of this image from many places in Nepal and Bhutan, and quite a collection from books and other research. And now—at last—I have a thangka for our shrine room.

PD: It is beautiful. I'm interested to see that you have had it framed in a wooden frame under glass, rather than in a traditional brocade frame. Why is that?

NN: It is quite a large painting and it would have made it a very large thangka with the addition of a brocade frame. As there are already quite a number of thangkas in our shrine room we are limited for space, so I decided to have it framed in a more European style.

PD The depictions of the Wheel of Life that I have seen in Nepal have been painted directly onto a wall rather than on cloth. Was that also a factor in choosing not to make a brocade frame?

NN: That is an interesting deduction – but no, that was not the reason for framing it this way. It would have been wonderful to have had it painted directly onto the wall, but perhaps it will have a longer life as a thangka in a frame.

PD: Am I correct in thinking that the Wheel of Life being painted on the *outside* of Buddhist buildings is a factor in your interest in it?

NN: Yes. I greatly appreciate that this image is always available for anyone to view. It is found at so many Buddhist sites – places where photography of the images *inside* their sacred buildings is forbidden, whereas photography is allowed of imagery on the *outside*. So it is always available to view and to photograph.

PD: And this has meant that you have been able to make a collection of several of these images?

NN: Yes… but my primary interest in the Wheel of Life as an image is that it is so iconic, has such detail, and tells a story.

PD: Tells a story?

NN: Yes, it is an image that you can read like a story. Anyone with a basic knowledge of Buddhism will be able to understand the message of this image.

1 – The Wheel of Life

Ngakpa 'ö-Dzin (N'ö): Thangkas used to be carried by monks who travelled from village to village giving teachings on the Wheel of Life. There is also a non-monastic Lama Mani tradition, of teaching through story telling.

PD: I guess that in Himalayan countries, where Buddhism is the foundation of people's spiritual background, the imagery of the Wheel of Life is familiar and understood?

NN: Yes.

PD: Perhaps it is not as easy to understand for people brought up in a different spiritual culture?

NN: Possibly not. People raised in a region with a spiritual background in another religion, would have to learn to *read* Buddhist imagery and symbolism.

PD: I can see that. Christianity has been part of the culture of Britain for more than a thousand years, so British culture is saturated with a basic Christian view and its imagery.

NN: Yes indeed – and I would say that I have felt this cultural relationship with Christianity especially strongly in the Welsh community.

PD: So Christianity permeates British culture even for people who are not practitioners?

N'ö: Yes. Also, those who regard themselves as Christians will display a broad spectrum of depth of involvement. So, for example, there may be those who go to church for midnight mass or a carol service at Christmas, but do not attend church services at any other time of year.

PD: Ah yes, and I know of people who do not attend church regularly, but will feel it important to turn to Christianity at key points in life, such as a wedding, a baptism, or a funeral.

1 – *The Wheel of Life*

NN: And many will try to live by the basic principles of Christianity, whilst not being practitioners as such.

PD: So are you suggesting that it is the same with Buddhism – and particularly with the imagery associated with Buddhism?

NN: Yes.

PD: So in the same way that someone brought up in Britain will immediately understand an image of a figure on a cross, a boat with pairs of animals, a baby in a manger, and so on, a person brought up in the Himalayan regions where Buddhism predominates will immediately recognise the images in the Wheel of Life – that this is part of the basic imagery of Himalayan Buddhism and will therefore be recognisable to anyone brought up in that context?

NN: Exactly. It represents the basic Buddhist teachings.

PD: The basic teachings featured in The Wheel of Life are the teachings of Sutra which came from Shakyamuni Buddha…?

NN: That is correct.

PD: But our Lineage—the Aro gTér—is a Vajrayana lineage, so why does this image interest you so much?

NN: Any teaching can be *read* from the perspective of another vehicle.

PD: The topic of the vehicles is complicated.

NN: It is. That is true.

PD: I know that in the Nyingma Tradition there are nine vehicles: three encompass Sutra and six encompass Tantra.

N'ö: The term we will use is *Vajrayana*, which refers to the practices of the six Tantras – the three Outer Tantras and the Three Inner Tantras.

NN: In the Nyingma tradition, the term *Sutrayana* is used to refer to the three vehicles of Shravakabuddhayana, Pratyekabuddhayana and Bodhisattvabuddhayana. The goal of Sutrayana is the realisation of emptiness.

PD: What about the terms *Sutra, Tantra* and *Dzogchen*?

NN: This is the three vehicle approach of Dzogchen, when the sixth Tantra—atiyoga or Dzogchen—is regarded as a vehicle in its own right.

N'ö: For the purposes of looking at this teaching, it will be sufficient to use the terms Sutrayana and Vajrayana.

PD: So, if I may ask again, as a Vajrayana practitioner, why would you go back to Sutrayana?

NN: To regard it as *going back* would be a sequentialist view: that you practise Sutrayana, and then Vajrayana. The understanding gained from Sutrayana is not discarded when you begin practising Vajrayana. Even if you *begin* as a Vajrayana practitioner, you *will* learn the Sutrayana teachings as well, even if you do not base your practice in that path. The important point is to practise whatever is most appropriate for the situation in which you find yourself. Having an understanding of the Sutrayana teachings is most valuable.

PD: I can see that teachings on impermanence and death—as an example—are always relevant.

NN: Yes indeed. What matters is how you are in the world. If it is not possible in the heat of the moment, to find emptiness and employ Vajrayana method, it is important to be honest about this. In order to avoid hurting others, sometimes a response of patience and letting go is needed, or of deciding to apply an opponent method, such as actively being generous when you are feeling greedy. This is a Sutrayana approach. The skilful practitioner understands that Sutrayana is valuable and appropriate at times, and is always available as an option.

PD: So… if I understand what you are saying… if I'm angry, and cannot transform the anger into clarity, then it is better to practise a Sutrayana approach rather than to risk expressing the anger and hurting someone? So I could count to 10, walk away, or think of something friendly to say. Is that what you mean?

NN: Yes. Absolutely. Ngak'chang Rinpoche has often said that he did not lose weight by employing Vajrayana – he practised Sutrayana: renunciation. Sometimes renunciation is the appropriate practice.

PD: That is a marvellous example! So practical and down to earth.

N'ö: Buddhism is often very pragmatic.

PD: I have heard that all the vehicles can be viewed from the perspective of each other. So does this mean that the Sutrayana teaching of the Wheel of Life can be viewed from the perspective of Vajrayana?

NN: Yes. When we look at it in detail we can find out.

PD: That will be very interesting. Now… you said that the Wheel of Life is available to everyone, being on the outside of Buddhist buildings… what would be a good term for a Buddhist building?

N'ö: *Lhakhang* is a good word. It covers many different places of Buddhist practice.

PD: Thank you. So the image is on the outside of the lhakhang, so everyone can learn something from it. Is this what appeals to you?

NN: Yes, that is certainly part of my personal fascination with the Wheel of Life. I appreciate the structure and details of the image and its message. I like the simplicity and logic of the Sutrayana teachings expressed in the painting. I do not have to abandon that appreciation because I practise Vajrayana. I love an illustrated story.

PD: Doesn't Vajrayana have its own logic?

NN: Yes it does – of course. But the logic of Vajrayana may not be so immediately accessible, because it plays with paradox, ambiguity and confusion. Vajrayana dances with knowing and not knowing. It uses symbolic method and requires a leap beyond ordinary view.

PD: So does Vajrayana require a more advanced practitioner?

NN: No, that's not really the point. Vajrayana is within the capacity of ordinary people, but some degree of experience of emptiness is required – and a relationship with a teacher is essential. Vajrayana is direct and works with the colour, texture and circumstances of ordinary life exactly as it is.

PD: So monasticism is the Sutrayana approach?

NN: Quite – although monastics certainly also practise symbolic Vajrayana.

N'ö: Vajrayana is personal – it works with how you are as an individual. A teacher is needed to enable the student to do that. In contrast, the teachings of Sutrayana can be generally applied for everyone – they are not individual in the same way.

PD: But a Sutrayana practitioner will still have a teacher…

NN: Yes, but the teacher is the spiritual friend who guides the student through the Sutras. The teacher does not use personality—theirs or the student's—as a method of teaching.

PD: But the Vajrayana teacher works in an individual way with the student and personality is part of that?

NN: Yes.

PD: Is that why Sutrayana is said to be a long and gradual path and Vajrayana is faster?

NN: Yes.

N'ö: Regarding all methods as always available demands authentic awareness of where you are in the moment. It is respectful of all teachings and practices. It enables real kindness, compassion, joyous empathy and equanimity to be the base of how you are in your life and of how you interact with everyone and everything, everywhere.

PD: So the Wheel of Life is found on the outside of the lhakhang. Is there more to say on the significance of this?

NN: Everyday visitors at a lhakhang may not wish to go inside – or feel they should not. They may only go inside the lhakhang to attend an event or ceremony on special days. It is a common practice for Himalayan Buddhists to circumambulate a lhakhang as a practice. They may recite mantra or make prostrations whilst doing this.

PD: Yes I have seen this a lot in Nepal – people walking with a rosary or spinning a prayer wheel.

N'ö: Families may also spend time together at a lhakhang.

PD: Yes. I noticed that as well. There are prostration boards in front of the Great Chörten in Kathmandu, and there were often family groups there. I also noticed that there were often quite a number of elderly people. This was particularly noticeable in the gardens at the Memorial Chörten in Thimphu, Bhutan.

NN: That's right. It is a common practice in these communities for older people to enter into spiritual practice assiduously in their later years, once they are no longer responsible for household duties and supporting their family. For example, the elderly father of one family we have known quite well in Nepal dedicates his time to studying Dharma and practising. When visiting the shop run by his daughter, Tenzin Dölma, he would often be there reading a pecha. We knew him as 'A-pha', which just means 'father'. When I attended a tshogs'khorlo at a Nyingma lhakhang in Bodhanath, this gentleman was received with great respect and reverence.

PD: In our culture, it is perhaps more common for the elderly to try to hang on to the activities of their younger days, rather than regarding their final years as an opportunity to engage in spiritual practice.

NN: That is true. Retirement may be regarded as a perpetual vacation – until sickness, old age and death prevent it.

PD: That seems to be a bit of shame when life expectancy can be reasonably hoped to extend into one's eighties—or even nineties—nowadays.

N'ö: Yes indeed. Retirement could be regarded as a great opportunity. There could be the possibility of ten, fifteen, or even twenty years of dedicated spiritual practice at this end of life.

PD: Returning to the Wheel of Life… is this the point of it being on the outer walls of the lhakhang – it is there for all visitors to see?

NN: That has always been my supposition. Parents and grandparents can talk to children about the image. There may be a monk or a yogic practitioner available to answer questions. In this way the basic principles of Buddhism can be taught, and understanding deepened.

PD: So the Wheel of Life being on the outside of the lhakhang is quite important. I remember how some of the lhakhangs are not very accessible at all if you are elderly or infirm. The steps up to some of the lhakhangs in Bhutan are more like a ladder than a staircase. I found them quite challenging at times.

NN: Yes. I found the same. So painting a teaching on the outside of the lhakhang is therefore an act of great kindness.

PD: Another thing I noticed when visiting a lhakhang, was that a large number of the local community might be present when a ceremony was taking place, such as a tshogs'khorlo, or a performance of cham. What surprised me though, is that they would be sitting at the back chatting to each other, and not appearing to follow or join in with the practice at all.

N'ö: This is cultural.

PD: I found it rather extraordinary.

N'ö: They feel that it is beneficial to be there. They make an offering to the lhakhang and might receive a blessing from the Lama, or one of the senior practitioners. This is the way they involve themselves in being Buddhists.

PD: I see. It did seem that this situation was perfectly normal and acceptable to those engaged in the practice and to the Lama on the high throne. No one told them to be quiet or anything like that.

NN: The local community are there through respect for Buddhism and to support those you could call the *professional practitioners* – those who are actually performing the ritual. These professional practitioners may be monks or nuns, or members of the go-kar-chang-lo'i de: ngakpas and ngakmas, naljorpas and naljormas.

PD: So might these members of the ordinary community not practise at all, other than attending events at the lhakhang?

N'ö: That is impossible to answer. It will vary from person to person. They may have a shrine at home, and make offerings. They may practise circumambulation. They may practise prostrations and mantra recitation. These aspects of Buddhist practice may be a natural part of their ordinary life, but they may not practise to any serious degree until the later years of their lives.

PD: So attending a ritual practice in this manner is culturally normal?

NN: Yes.

PD: It seems to me that perhaps people who convert to Buddhism from another spiritual background take it more seriously. They are more likely to actually engage in practice.

NN: That is making a value judgement based on your cultural norms. Chatting at the back of the lhakhang whilst a ritual is being performed does not demonstrate a lack of respect or a lack of seriousness about being a Buddhist. Being there, supporting the professional practitioners, and holding Buddhism as their spiritual ground *is* taking it seriously.

PD: But Westerners who convert to Buddhism do seem to actually practise.

NN: Well that would be the reason for converting – because of an interest in actively practising that religion.

PD: But perhaps the people chatting at the back of the lhakhang will expect to dedicate a lot of time to practice later in life?

NN: Yes, that is entirely possible.

PD: Has every lhakhang you have visited in Nepal and Bhutan had this image on a wall outside?

NN: I couldn't say I've seen it at *every* lhakhang – but that might just be that I didn't happen to come across it. They are not always on the outer wall by the main entrance. I have seen it at the majority of lhakhangs. There are also often other images on the outside, such as the symbols of longevity, guardians of the four directions, and astrological symbols.

PD: I see. What do you think is the primary message of the Wheel of Life?

NN: Firstly, that you *are* going to die – this is certain. Then, that you create your own reality through your perceptions and responses. And also, that you need to be aware of the consequences of those perceptions and responses – that they may be the cause of an uncomfortable rebirth.

PD: Those are weighty considerations!

NN: They certainly are, and they are relevant to everyone everywhere.

PD: Could we just run through the different sections of the Wheel of Life?

NN: Sure.

PD: The outer rim describes the twelve links of interdependent origination?

NN: Yes.

PD: Then there are six sections – the realms where you can take rebirth.

NN: Correct.

PD: Then there is a circle showing the bad going down to the hell realms, and the good going up to heaven.

NN: Well I would not describe that ring in quite that way, but we can discuss that when we look at the different sections in detail.

PD: Yes. Okay. Then in the centre there is a bird, a snake and a pig chasing each other, which is an illustration of cycling through patterning.

NN: That will suffice for now, but again I would not explain the central hub in quite those terms. One thing you did not mention is that the Wheel itself is being held by the Lord of Death.

PD: Oh yes. I suppose that is an important aspect – as important as the details of the actual Wheel.

N'ö: Certainly.

PD: Why do you think it is a wheel?

NN: Good question! The wheel is ancient. It dates back to about 3000 BCE. Interestingly, as there is an illustration of a potter in the outer rim of the Wheel, it is thought that the first wheels were used by potters, and then only later for transportation.

PD: So a wheel is used as a symbol because it would be well understood by anyone looking at it – as something that moves in a circular manner?

NN: Yes, that is right. It is a clear depiction of a cycle – something that turns and turns. It is also a practical symbol that can be easily divided into sections.

PD: I think that people also understand momentum in relation to a wheel – that it will continue to roll unless something happens to stop it.

N'ö: Absolutely. All these factors make it a potent symbol even before we start to look at the details.

PD: So can we go through the details of the Wheel section by section?

NN: Certainly – but I think this is enough for this session.

PD: When we start our next session, should we begin our examination of the Wheel of Life from the outside of the Wheel or from the centre?

NN: Aha! Another good question! Either could be argued as a perfectly sensible approach. Personally, I think I would start at the outside and move inwards.

PD: That's fine by me. I am looking forward to discovering all the details of this beautiful thangka. It will be so much easier to see and discuss all the details with this thangka here to look at closely. Images in books are usually rather too small to decipher.

NN: I have also created some line drawings based on the thangka to make it easier to see some of the small details.

PD: Oh great. I look forward to seeing those as well.

NN: Good. So let's do that.

PD: So in the morning, we can start at the outside and move towards the centre. Thank you. It will be fun.

NN: It will… but now I'm sure you must be tired after your journey, so let's go and have a hot drink and retire for the night. The bed in the spare room is made up ready for you.

N'ö: We hope you will be comfortable. Let us know if there is anything you need.

PD: Thank you very much.

Yama
Lord of Death

2 – Yama Lord of Death

Saturday morning dawns. Ngakma Nor'dzin, Ngakpa 'ö-Dzin, and Pema Dorje have returned to the shrineroom after morning practice and breakfast. They sit in silence for a few minutes, gazing into space. Then they sing **A** *for the length of a breath. After a few more moments of silence, they smile at each other and return to their seats in front of the thangka of the Wheel of Life, ready to continue their discussion.*

PD: One cannot help but notice—when first seeing the Wheel of Life—that it is held by a fierce and frightening being. I believe this is Yama, the Lord of Death?

NN: It is – Yama Dharmaraja or Shinje Chögyal. Yama is *frightening*, but his purpose as guardian of the Wheel of Life is to inspire a sense of urgency rather than trying to actually cause fear. Fear is generally counterproductive because it leads to self-protectiveness.

N'ö: Yama is not *threatening* anyone – just alerting the viewer to the very real and immediate threat of impermanence and death. He is offering a warning and a reminder. He is urging direct recognition of reality – especially the reality that the death of this life could happen at any moment, and that the death of the present moment is continual.

PD: I see. That is an important message. There can be a tendency to ignore the reality of impermanence. Life seems to create a certain complacency.

NN: Indeed it does. The manner and visage of Yama—and of all the wrathful awareness beings—reminds me of an incident many years ago when our boys were little. We were at a Bonfire Night celebration with friends and family.

PD: I haven't been to a Bonfire Night celebration in years.

NN: It is the same for us. Nowadays we rarely do anything on Bonfire Night, but for children it can be a magical experience. It is fun—as a child—to be allowed to stay up late and stand around a bonfire, wrapped up warmly. Fireworks are always enjoyable and bonfire food is a bit special: potatoes wrapped in foil and cooked in the bonfire embers, and marshmallows roasted on long sticks.

N'ö: For most people, Bonfire Night is simply an incendiary celebration, rather than a remembrance of an historical event.

PD: So what happened at the Bonfire Night with your brother that reminded you of wrathful awareness beings?

NN: Well, the bonfire was a little reluctant to get going. My brother's partner had a bottle of paraffin beside her. It had been used to help the first sticks to catch fire. She picked up the bottle of paraffin and started to unscrew the lid. Fortunately Ngakpa-la noticed and understood what she was about to do. He leapt towards her shouting, "NO!" before she got as far as actually throwing the paraffin onto the fire. He was instantly energised. He moved with athletic immediacy, and the urgency and authority in his voice could not be ignored or disobeyed.

PD: Wow.

N'ö: Yes it was quite a dangerous moment.

NN: I remember how your whole demeanour changed as you leapt towards her, incisively direct in the moment of needing to stop her throwing the paraffin.

N'ö: Had she thrown it, it could have been an unpleasant, painful, and potentially life-changing disaster for her. The paraffin would have caught fire, and the flame would have shot back along the flow of liquid to the bottle in her hand.

PD: Oh my. That would have been bad. I've seen stories of that sort of thing in the news. There always seem to be a few accidents like that every Bonfire Night.

NN: Quite. The urgency and immediacy that was needed in that moment, is—for me—like the directness and energy of wrathful beings. Here, it is Yama, the Lord of Death. He is shouting, '*STOP! Remember death! Remember that everything ends! Recognise self-created suffering! Cease turning the Wheel of Life!*'

PD: So he has that fierce athletic urgency and command that you recognised in Ngakpa-la responding to danger?

NN: Exactly. Yama has completely recognised the reality of the situation and wishes to prevent disaster. He is wrathfully present and direct. His presence and directness is a warning, an energetic instruction to take notice and wake up. He is warning the viewer to wake up to the reality of death and impermanence.

N'ö: Life and death are inextricably interwoven. To ignore death—as a continual manifestation in life—is to be asleep. To be asleep is to be trapped within the Wheel – unaware of being trapped, and unaware of the need and possibility of escape.

PD: So is Yama a warning that the Wheel of Cyclic Existence has been turning for eternity, and will keep turning forever unless action is taken to stop it?

NN: Absolutely. The turning of the Wheel is the eternal cycle of seeking satisfaction and failing to find it – because the nature and source of both satisfaction and dissatisfaction are misunderstood.

PD: Actually though… looking at the thangka… Yama is *holding* the Wheel…?

NN: Well observed. Yama holds the Wheel tightly. He holds it so tightly and definitely that he even has it in his teeth.

PD: So is the message that he has stopped the Wheel?

NN: That could be one way of interpreting it: that he has stopped the Wheel to show the pattern – to enable the viewer to examine what is going on. He is holding it stationary – so that anyone and everyone can wake up and understand the mechanism of cyclic existence.

PD: It is like a pause – a moment in time that can be examined.

N'ö: Yes. Yama is offering a present moment of awareness for us to look at. The present moment is continually ignored because of addiction to analysis.

PD: Addiction to analysis?

N'ö: Everything is classified with reference to past experience, and that analysis is projected into the future as expectation. Direct experience becomes impossible because of this continual referentiality.

PD: So in this moment of stillness that Yama is offering, the whole pattern of cyclic existence can be viewed?

NN: Yes. Understanding the story described in the Wheel of Life imagery, enables the truth of the experience of dissatisfaction to become evident. The cause of dissatisfaction is explained. The possibility of ending dissatisfaction is illustrated, and the possibility of discovering the path that leads to the end of dissatisfaction is revealed.

PD: That sounded like the Four Noble Truths…?

NN: Yes. I sneaked them in there!

PD: So the Wheel expresses that we experience dissatisfaction and shows the cause; and also teaches that the Wheel can be stopped and how to do that?

NN: Yes.

PD: I seem to remember there is a legend about Yama – that he was a holy man who believed that he would gain enlightenment if he meditated in a cave for 50 years. During the 11th month of the 49th year, robbers appeared in his cave, dragging a stolen bull. They cut off the bull's head. Then they noticed the holy man, and realised that he had seen them, so they attacked him and cut off his head as well. Being the 11th month of the 49th year of his practice, the holy man had considerable power, and was able to rise again. He didn't put his own head back on though, but rather the bull's head – and so assumed the terrible form of Yama. He then killed the robbers, drank their blood, and became a powerful demon who threatened all of Tibet.

N'ö: Eventually he was subdued and oath-bound as a dam-chan, a protector of Buddhism.

NN: It is a graphic tale. As an oath-bound protector he is a warning to practise Dharma or remain trapped in the cycle of the turning Wheel. The background in this thangka is simple and sparse, but often Yama, holding the Wheel of Life, is depicted standing in a natural environment where the natural elements are displayed. Yama stands on the solidity of the earth, in a landscape that is rich; he is himself substantial and impressive. Water is indicated by a pond, a stream, a waterfall, clouds and snowy mountain peaks. Fire is represented by daylight and the sun in the sky, and by Yama's energetic stance. Yama's body is a deep red, the colour of dried blood. He also has flaming eyebrows and a crown of flaming skulls. Air is symbolised by green foliage, and the lively plants and animals in the foreground. Yama wears a shawl—sometimes a green shawl—that is billowing in the wind. The whole image exists in its own space, and the deep blue of the sky is also a symbol of space.

PD: The natural elements are like a stage where the Wheel of Life turns.

NN: Yes. The elements are the essential building blocks of reality. Samsara—the continual cycling of dualistic existence—performs in this natural elemental environment. The performance does not affect the natural state of the elements.

PD: Ah yes – the distortion and dissatisfaction that are experienced are individual and self-created. The natural environment is unaffected and remains pristine.

N'ö: Absolutely. The stage remains perfect as it is. Performers do not pollute the stage as they appear – they only experience it as imperfect through their personal confusion. Performers appear, act out the patterns of individual confusion, and then disappear – only to appear again and repeat the patterning.

PD: Arising, abiding and experiencing, and then dissolving – it is endless.

NN: This is the nature of form. The *manner* of arising, abiding, and dissolving is individual. Whether this movement—the turning of the Wheel—is unwinding or consolidating patterning is individual. The Wheel of Life thangka is a teaching to enable the recognition of the continual cycling of dissatisfaction, and the continual creation and consolidation of the patterns of delusion and confusion. Yama—death—is holding the Wheel in his teeth and talons – holding it still so that this patterning can be examined.

PD: Is the stillness of Yama holding the Wheel itself a symbol?

NN: The stillness is emptiness.

PD: So although the teaching of cyclic existence is based in Sutrayana, the observer who has the capacity to see it can recognise the most subtle teaching of Vajrayana – the nonduality of form and emptiness.

NN: Yes. Buddhism is a religion of method and the methods vary according to what is appropriate to the student, and according to the student's capacity. Stillness is the empty space at the end of one cycle before another one begins.

PD: And Buddhist practice offers many methods of finding that stillness, that emptiness.

NN: Yes. It can be discovered through silent sitting meditation.

N'ö: It can be discovered in relation to the Teacher.

NN: And it can be discovered through life circumstances.

PD: So could the Wheel of Life thangka be used to help understand what is discovered in that stillness?

NN: Yes… but how that is effected will depend on the vehicle of practice. In our tradition—the Aro gTér Lineage, a Vajrayana Lineage—silent sitting is experiential practice, not analytical, so any analysis would happen outside of the meditation session itself.

PD: Could this be described as a difference between Sutrayana and Vajrayana – because analytical meditation is a primary feature in Sutrayana, and a means of discovering emptiness?

NN: Yes.

PD: So is this an example of gaining a different perspective depending on the vehicle? In Sutrayana, contemplating the meaning of the Wheel of Life *is* a meditation practice. In Vajrayana, perhaps recognising the teaching in the Wheel of Life could be immediate and direct because of experience of silent sitting without an analytical focus.

NN: Yes. Good. In meditation, the meditator can find the natural state of the elements; can find the natural state of Mind without distortion.

N'ö: The stillness offered by Yama can either be an opportunity to analyse, or an opportunity to experience *knowing* directly.

PD: *Knowing?*

NN: *Knowing* that is immediate and direct, and beyond intellect.

PD: Although there is stillness—because the Wheel has been stopped by Yama—the details of the Wheel are full of activity. Could this be understood as nonduality as well – the nonduality of form and emptiness?

NN: Absolutely. The nonduality of emptiness and form is the only *truth* in Buddhism. It will inevitably be there in every Buddhist teaching.

PD: I still don't understand why Yama has to be *such* a frightening image? The wrathful awareness beings are quite ugly and demonic.

NN: This sounds like a cultural bias – an interpretation based in the norms of your upbringing. It cannot be denied that Yama looks ferocious, but think of it as energy. It is the energy and capacity to act in a moment of danger – like stopping my brother's partner from setting fire to herself.

N'ö: If I had just sat there and said, '*You know that really isn't such a good idea…*' the action would have been completed before the message got through.

PD: Yes of course. I can see that.

N'ö: Yama is an energetic embodiment of urgency and immediacy – an embodiment of the need to recognise death.

NN: It could be said that we have spent lifetimes considering whether perhaps cyclic existence is not such a good idea… and consequently have burned ourselves over and over again. Yama's demeanour says: *NOW! AT ONCE! STOP!* He has to express urgency. He has to be impossible to ignore…

PD: … because people continually deny the reality of impermanence and death, whilst at the same time being continually afraid of impermanence and death.

NN: Exactly.

PD: Death is followed by birth, though – new form arises?

NN: That is true. In fact, being afraid of permanence and immortality would make just as much sense as being afraid of impermanence and death – but we are so addicted to form that this feels less frightening.

PD: Perhaps Yama is holding the Wheel still and proclaiming: *Aha! I have trapped you! You will remain in this form forever!* That could be just as terrifying.

NN: Indeed. That is a really useful way to look at it.

PD: So there is a contradictory relationship with form. People relish change when it is desired and looked forward to – such as a holiday, the birth of a baby, a new job, a change of hairstyle, shiny new shoes, or whatever…

NN: … but ignore the death that precedes the new form.

N'ö: Your comfy bed at home must be given up for a less comfortable hotel bed; the arrival of a baby is the death of the freedom to go out whenever you want; the new job is the death of the familiarity and friendships of the old job…

NN: … the new hairstyle is the death of identity caught up in the old hair style; and the new shoes are the death of the comfort of the old, scuffed shoes…

PD: We do tend to look at the potential for desirable new form and ignore the potential of *un*desirable new form. Looking at it the other way around, sometimes life provides circumstances that will not change however much it is wished that they would: the migraine headache, or stomach upset that lasts too long and will not cease; the annoying neighbour who will not stop their inconsiderate behaviour…

NN: These are all descriptions of cyclic existence. Yama encourages anyone who looks at him, holding the Wheel of Life in suspension, to look at these cycles: the birth and death of each moment, each wish, each aspiration, each irritation. He invites the viewer to look at when death is desired and when birth is desired – and when change happens whatever is desired, and when change fails to happen however much it is desired.

N'ö: Wanting to be in control is the source of the problem and Yama is the empty controller. The moment, situation, event, activity, emotion, dies when it dies. Yama does not kill it. He is simply the embodiment of the reality of its death.

PD: Ah, yes of course. That might be the crux of the matter. I see him as frightening because I blame death for loss, unwanted change, and so on, and forget that death is also the herald of meeting, gain, happy changes, and so on.

NN: You might recognise the oscillations of the eight worldly dharmas in that statement.

PD: Yes! Gain and loss; hope and fear; praise and blame; meeting and parting.

NN: You do not *own* your body and your life – and you are not in control of your circumstances. Consciousness has just taken up residence in this form for a while. A lifetime is a blink in a continuum.

N'ö: This time male… this time female. This time in Tibet… this time in Europe.

NN: This time your child… sibling… parent… friend… enemy… stranger. This time healthy… this time sick. This time tall… this time short. This time big strong body… this time slim athletic body.

N'ö: Death is a blip in the continuum – and immediately followed by birth. Death of that life and birth of this one.

PD: Am I correct in thinking, that this pause—Yama holding the Wheel—is also demanding that we look even more closely. That we look at the present moment. There is the death of that thought and the birth of this one… the death of that perception and the birth of this one… the death of that sensory experience and birth of this one…

NN: Absolutely.

PD: I have not had much experience of actual death – I mean, end-of-life death.

NN: Well that does not matter really – you cannot *get used* to death by being around it. But it can be useful to notice how things change, and I think living in this Close of eighteen houses has been useful for that.

PD: Useful in what way?

NN: Because this is a cul-de-sac, there is no passing traffic. No one comes into the Close unless they have a reason to. It is a quiet enclosure.

PD: It sounds like a nice place to live.

NN: It is.

N'ö: When we first moved into the Close it was a micro-community because nearly every resident had bought their property as a new-build. Not all of the residents were close friends, but they certainly all knew each other. Also the shape of the Close—an elongated circle of houses gathered around the road space—feels a bit like a tribe gathered around the fire. Everyone knows something about everyone else, even if only remotely. The comings and goings, changes and adjustments are witnessed in a way that is more intimate than it can be in a long row of houses.

PD: I can see that. It is possible to not know anything at all about a neighbour only a few doors away in a row of houses.

NN: That had been our experience before moving here. The Close has enabled us to naturally witness the changing face of a community. It has been an opportunity to observe the ebb and flow of life and death. Children have grown up and left home. Some have returned to live in the Close as adults. People who lived here as children, now bring *their* children to visit. Several deaths have created a change of ownership. Some deaths have been long and drawn out into old age. Others have been sudden and dramatic. So Yama's presence in the Close—as a director of change, life and death—impels us to remember the urgency of the present moment.

PD: I think that is also an example of how everything can be embraced as practice, if you are open to that possibility.

NN: Exactly.

PD: Something has just occurred to me… could the Wheel be understood as a mirror?

NN: Yes, it could. The Wheel reflects reality. It shows us how our lives circle and circle through perpetual striving for satisfaction using the familiar processes described in the details of the Wheel.

N'ö: Yama—in holding the Wheel—suggests that in this infinite, eternal, rolling, timeless continuity there is a stillness – the stillness of *now*; the stillness of the present moment. This stillness is an opportunity to savour the present moment exactly as it is, free of striving. Yama demands that we have the courage to stop turning the Wheel of Samsara, and directly experience and appreciate everything exactly as it is.

NN: Quite… and I think that is a good place to end this session. Let's have a tea break and make a start on lunch preparation, and come back in a little while.

The Blank Canvas

3 – The Blank Canvas

It is late morning, and teachers and student have reconvened. They are once again sitting in front of the thangka of the Wheel of Life.

NN: So, here we are again, ready to start looking at the details of the Wheel itself.

PD: The outer circle of the Wheel is a series of small pictures that illustrate the twelve interdependent links of origination.

NN: Correct.

PD: I find this the most difficult part of the Wheel of Life to understand. The explanations I have read all suggest that the links describe at least one lifetime – and sometimes up to three lifetimes. The thing I find the most confusing however, is that there are ten links before the one that clearly shows a baby being born, and this is followed immediately by the last link: death! So how can this describe a lifetime? Why are there so many links before *birth*?

NN: *[Laughs]* Yes indeed – but you do not need to be concerned about that. We are examining the links from the perspective of Vajrayana, because that is where our practice is based in the Aro gTér Lineage. In terms of Vajrayana the twelve interdependent links are not describing the span of one life or several lives; they are not describing the span of a past, present or future life. You can just let go of that confusion.

PD: Oh really? That is a relief. Just forget about trying to fit the links into a human lifespan?

NN: Yes. That is one way of viewing the interdependent links. Teachers teach from their experience of practice, and from the vehicle in which they base their practice. In Vajrayana especially, commentary on the teachings can be highly individual to the teacher.

N'ö: The gradualist view of Sutrayana will tend towards the one life, or several lives analysis of the interdependent links. In Vajrayana the view is different.

NN: It is important that the images are the teaching. Understanding will arise depending on your practice, capacity, and the teaching you have received. It is important to avoid looking at it the other way round and trying to make what you know fit the images.

PD: Yes. I always felt I was doing the *trying-to-make-it-fit* with the several-lifetimes approach. I think that is why I never really understood the teaching of the links or found it useful to my practice and understanding. Am I correct in thinking that we start at the top with the old person and the child?

NN: The links are not numbered. Occasionally a wall painting of the Wheel of Life will have labels—such as the one at the lhakhang we stayed at in Bartsham in East Bhutan—but these give the name of the links without a number. It *is* usual to start with *ignorance* and this *is* usually at the top, but not always.

PD: So should we start somewhere other than at the top?

NN: Well the earliest source I have found for a teaching on the twelve interdependent links is the Rice Seedling Sutra. In this, Sariputra asks Maitreya to explain the teaching that had been given earlier by the Buddha to his monks. This teaching begins with ignorance and is perfectly clear about the order. Let me just quote this passage:

> *That is to say, ignorance causes formations. Formations cause consciousness. Consciousness causes name and form. Name and form cause the six sense sources. The six sense sources cause contact. Contact causes sensation. Sensation causes craving. Craving causes appropriation. Appropriation causes becoming. Becoming causes birth. And birth causes ageing and death, sorrow, lamentation, suffering, despair, and anxiety. Thus does this entire great heap of suffering arise.* Sutra of the Rice Seedling—stanza 1.4—84000: Translating the Words of the Buddha

PD: Yes, that is clear. And so it always goes clockwise?

NN: I cannot definitively answer that question. I am not an academic. I am a practitioner. The structure of the Wheel of Life image and its explanation can become extraordinarily complicated if you try to encompass every form of it that has appeared through the ages. Robert Beer, a well-respected author and thangka painter, told me that the most ancient known image of the Wheel of Life is in Ajanta in India and appears to have 18 interdependent links. You can find photographs of it. Unfortunately it is very damaged, but it also appears to have eight realms rather than six. It could become an interesting life's work to explore all the different forms of the Wheel, but in terms of *practice* that might not be the most beneficial use of one's time.

N'ö: I have read commentaries that describe the links in an anti-clockwise direction as the unwinding of the causes of cyclic existence. We have never received this teaching, however, and therefore cannot comment on it.

PD: I understand what you are saying. Academic exploration should be a support to practice, but not override practice.

NN: Exactly. So we have a thangka here, that is an image in *this form*, in *this place*, for *this time*. We can appreciate and use this image—and our knowledge of other Wheel of Life images—to support our understanding. This image can nourish our practice if we embrace it in that way.

PD: Thank you. I can see that my desire to get everything neatly sorted out and categorised is not helpful. So shall we begin?

N'ö: Of course, there is another reason why the teaching on the interdependent links is difficult to grasp.

PD: Oh yes?

N'ö: The links begin with fundamental ignorance: the belief in a self-existing 'I'.

PD: Is this what is indicated by a the person at the top with a child?

N'ö: Yes.

PD: Why is *this* symbol used here, whereas in the centre of the Wheel the symbol for ignorance is a pig?

NN: That is a good question. The pig in the central hub *does* represent ignorance – but a different type of ignorance. The pig is the wilful *ignorance* of anything that does not seem to challenge or support the delusion of a self-existing 'I'. Here—in the first link—ignorance *is* the delusion of an inherent and self-existing 'I' – the ignorance that starts everything. This fundamental delusion is the basis for all experience of dissatisfaction and the cause of all suffering.

N'ö: Perhaps we should take a few moments to look at this topic in detail, as it is essential to understanding the nonduality of self and lack-of-self, and the view of Vajrayana.

PD: Yes, please do say more. It is a difficult topic to grasp,

NN: Belief in an inherent, self-existing 'I' is an attempt to fix form, and deny emptiness. It is the basis of duality.

N'ö: There can be a tendency to be complacent about understanding impermanence: *yes, of course everything continually changes; things arise, things end – of course I understand that.* But hidden behind this intellectual understanding is an unspoken: *this applies to everything – except ME…*

NN: … except for that sense of being a someone and a something that is real, does not change, is unique, will continue forever and will always be clearly defined as ME.

PD: Yes, I can see that. So this is what is meant by the *self-existing I*?

NN: Yes. Yet the ME that we feel so strongly is also non-dual – it is inseparable emptiness and form.

N'ö: Ngak'chang Rinpoche suggested that emptiness could be understood as the blank wall—or canvas—on which the Wheel of Life is painted. The painting depends on the empty space on which it can appear.

NN: The painting appears on the wall, but is an ornament of the wall. The painting is not the wall itself.

N'ö: Identity arises and is experienced through physicality, energy, and awareness. The sense of identity—of I/ME/MINE—is not the actual reality of that physicality, energy, and awareness.

NN: Identity *can* be recognised in a moment of time – but then it is gone and has changed in the next moment. It is the attempt to hang on to a particular definition as a permanent state that causes problems.

PD: Is there also something in this about interpretation?

NN: Yes indeed. Present moment experience is interpreted through *what happened in the past; what is actually happening now*, and *projection based on past and present experience*. Dissatisfaction is experienced through attempting to carry the definition of ME through that.

PD: Rather than experiencing what is actually happening now directly?

NN: Yes.

N'ö: Perhaps an example would be useful? I will be meeting J— tomorrow. My previous experience of J— was that they were rude and unfriendly. I hold that past experience, and feel the need to protect myself from the likelihood of J— being rude and unfriendly again – so I project a protective response onto the future meeting. This approach to a situation will prevent the possibility of a direct and clear, fresh and unprejudiced experience of the meeting with J—. They will sense my protective/agressive stance, and this will influence how they are with me. Thus a whole mess of potential dissatisfaction is created through patterned response.

PD: So we should try to be a blank canvas and let the form that arises in the moment be whatever it is, without prejudice or projection?

NN: Exactly. The self is described as *illusory* because it exists, but not as a fixed, unchanging reality. A self exists in the moment that can perceive and respond, but the self that exists in *each* moment is a new self in *each* moment. Any sense of permanence and continuity is illusory. Perhaps Ngakpa-la would read a few more quotations from the Sutra of the Rice Seedling to help our understanding?

N'ö: It will be my pleasure:

> ... *the seed does not think, 'I form the sprout.' Nor does the sprout think, 'I am formed by the seed.' Likewise, the flower does not think, 'I form the fruit.' Nor does the fruit think, 'I am formed by the flower.'* Sutra of the Rice Seedling—stanza 1.12—84000: Translating the Words of the Buddha

> *(But) when the inner earth element is not deficient, and likewise the elements of water, fire, wind, space, and consciousness are not deficient, then from the coming together of all these factors, the body forms.* Sutra of the Rice Seedling—stanza 1.26—84000: Translating the Words of the Buddha

> *The earth element is not a self, not a being, not a life force, not a creature, not a human, not a person, not female, not male, not neuter, not me, not mine, and not anybody else's. Similarly, the water element, the fire element, the wind element, the space element, and the consciousness element are also not a self, not a being, not a life force, not a creature, not a human, not a person, not female, not male, not neuter, not me, not mine, and not anybody else's.* Sutra of the Rice Seedling—stanza 1.28—84000: Translating the Words of the Buddha

PD: These somehow remind me of the Heart Sutra.

NN: That is not surprising. We could look at a section of that Sutra:

> *"Form is not different from emptiness, emptiness is not different from form. That which seems like emptiness is form, and that which seems like form is emptiness. You will not find emptiness apart from form; or form apart from emptiness.*
>
> *The psychology of duality—sensation, thought, connection and consciousness—these are also both emptiness and form. So Shariputra, you can only characterise form in terms of emptiness; and you can only characterise emptiness in terms of form.*
>
> *The phenomena of reality are not existent, nor are they non-existent; they are not pure, nor are they impure; they do not increase, neither do they decrease. Psychological attributes are neither existent, nor non-existent. The perceptions of eyes, ears, nose, tongue, body, and mind are both reality and illusion; likewise form, sound, colour, taste, touch, objects; likewise the dimension of vision and awareness.*
>
> *There is no understanding and no absence of understanding. There is no suffering, old age, or death, nor do they end. There is no merit, nor lack of merit. There is no accumulation, no annihilation, no path, and no wisdom. There is no realisation or non-realisation. There is no attainment or absence of attainment.* The Heart Sutra – this extract is taken from the translation of its essential meaning by Ngak'chang Rinpoche.

PD: So, ignorance is the start of everything. Ignorance of reality causes the cycle of the links to start rolling?

NN: Yes.

PD: How can we let go of this ignorance? The sense of a self is so strong.

N'ö: Through practice – especially silent sitting.

NN: We have to get used to emptiness. We have to learn how to see the emptiness of each thought, sensation, idea, memory, and so on – recognise the temporary state of experience and definition. As emptiness becomes less threatening and more familiar, the illusory nature of phenomena is perceived.

N'ö: And eventually this will include recognising the illusory nature of our sense of a self-identity. We can recognise that identity arises in the moment and may change in the next moment.

PD: So this is part of the understanding of Yama holding the Wheel still? That the image on the blank canvas—the scenes depicted in the Wheel—are a moment in time?

NN: Absolutely. Remembering this will increase your insight into the teaching of the Wheel at each level.

PD: Yes. I can see how it will.

NN: But *this* moment in time is defined as *Lunchtime*. We'll have a break and come back refreshed to look at all the interdependent links in detail.

Links of Causation

4 – Links of Causation

It is Saturday afternoon. Ngakma Nor'dzin, Ngakpa 'ö-Dzin and Pema Dorje have enjoyed lunch and a short walk to stretch their legs and get some fresh outdoor air.

N'ö: So now we are ready for an in-depth discussion of the twelve links. Once again we start at the top with *ignorance*.

NN: Yes. I think a good way to start is to simply look at the pictures and feel your way into their meaning. The images *do* have the capacity to *speak* to the viewer, without the need of a long and erudite translation full of technical language. Allow them to tell their story.

PD: It can be expected that they tell their story because this is an image that is always available outside the lhakhang, available for anyone and everyone to see?

NN: Yes – as we discussed earlier.

N'ö: The style of the image and the basic message would be well known by anyone brought up in the Himalayan region.

PD: The links seem quite complicated compared to the other images on the Wheel, but perhaps the message could actually be quite simple?

NN: Yes, indeed. The images must be able to tell their story. So shall we start by just looking at the twelve images as they are – without too much interpretation of their meaning? I will also show you my illustrations taken from the thangka. Let's start with the person at the top with a stick, accompanied by a child.

PD: Great. Thanks.

NN: What does this image show?

Travelling at the Speed of Mind

PD: There is an elderly person with a walking stick who seems to be being encouraged to go back rather than forward by a child.

NN: You are correct about the clockwise direction of the links, according to the Rice Seedling Sutra, but your extrapolation that therefore these figures in the first link are 'going back' is not correct. There is not a sense of going backwards here. Sometimes the child and elderly person are depicted facing in the other direction. It is just that they have been painted facing to the left in this thangka.

PD: I see.

N'ö: If this thangka was using European symbolism, the stick would be white and be being held out in front.

PD: Ah, so the person is blind.

NN: Yes.

N'ö: The next image is of a potter surrounded by the pots that they have made.

PD: I like this image. Something is being created.

NN: Very good. How about the next link?

PD: This is a monkey clambering over a building.

N'ö: It seems to be more common for the monkey to be in a tree, but in this thangka it is indeed scampering over a building.

PD: For me, a monkey is a very lively image. Monkeys are agile and skilful, and in their element swinging from tree to tree or—I liked your word—scampering over a building. Monkeys can also be quite unruly, excitable and mischievous.

N'ö: Yes indeed. Do you remember the monkeys in Nepal? They were quick and clever. They would steal your lunch in the blink of an eye and be up in the top of a tree before you could even shout at them.

NN: *[Laughs]* Oh yes... So what follows our excitable monkey?

PD: The next one is an image of a boat with four people in it.

NN: What does that say to you?

PD: A boat is a means of transport, so these people are on a journey. It might be some sort of ferry, because the man with the oars is dressed differently whilst the passengers all look the same. In fact they all look like some sort of religious folk.

NN: We can discuss that aspect later. What do you make of the next one: a house with six windows?

PD: A house is a solid structure, somewhere to set up home. It protects you from the weather, and makes life more comfortable.

NN: All true. What's it like to be inside?

4 – Links of Causation

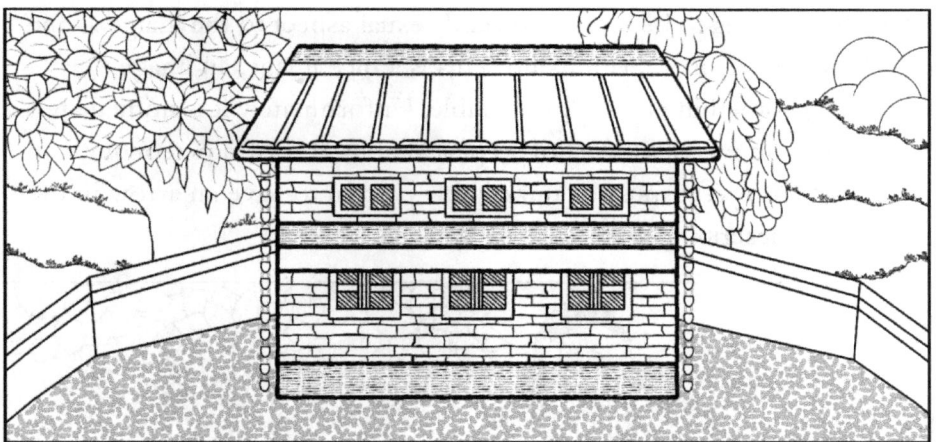

PD: Ah yes – it is important to personalise these images. If I'm in the house, I am limited to experiencing what is outside the house via the windows. This will make me less directly connected with the outside world.

NN: Yes indeed. It is usually said that it is an empty house – but again we can return to explanations later. The next image is of a couple. In this thangka they are in bed together, but in some thangkas they are just embracing, commonly sitting under a tree.

PD: There is intimacy in this image, possibly the first intimacy?

NN: Yes.

PD: There seems to be a romantic and sexual aspect to the image as the couple are clearly in a relationship. This is a nice image, an image expressing something that is pleasurable. Unfortunately it is immediately followed by an image that is not so pleasurable. It is of a person with an arrow in their eye. It must be unbearably painful to have an arrow in the eye. This is describing an intense experience.

NN: Quite. Intense is exactly the right word.

N'ö: Then the next image is more pleasurable again.

PD: Yes. It is a person being served a drink. I would guess that this is an alcoholic drink, as they are in front of a building, which is perhaps an alehouse. There is a feeling of the drinking being enjoyable.

4 – *Links of Causation*

NN: Quite so. Then in this thangka the next picture is of a person picking fruit from a tree, surrounded by baskets full of fruit. In other thangkas I have seen this link illustrated as a monkey in a tree grasping a piece of fruit.

PD: This seems quite straightforward. The fruit is nourishing and available, and being harvested. I think it must be significant that it is an edible substance that is being gathered. This and the previous picture both depict things that can be consumed.

NN: Good point. Then we move away from this theme…

Travelling at the Speed of Mind

PD: I don't understand this one from the thangka. It is just a standing woman.

NN: Yes it is not always easy to recognise the detail in these small images around the edge of the thangka. Can you make anything more out of my illustration? I have emphasised the details a little.

PD: She is a married woman – we know that from her apron. I think she looks as though she is pregnant.

NN: Correct. Some thangkas show a couple making love for this link, but I suppose the thangka painter felt that he had used that image already.

PD: So this is illustrating the conception of a new life, or the actual pregnancy. Then the next image is the inevitable outcome of conception and pregnancy: the birth of a baby. This is a rather graphic image of a woman giving birth.

4 – *Links of Causation*

NN: *[Laughs]* Yes. I have always appreciated the directness of the depiction of this link. Some thangkas are even more graphic than this one with quite a lot of blood coming from the mother and on the baby.

N'ö: In this thangka the woman is alone, but it is more usual for her to have an attendant, so Ngakma-la added a figure to her illustration.

PD: I find this to be quite a potent image.

NN: Yes indeed. Giving birth is a potent experience. I remember one day in the third trimester of my first pregnancy, suddenly having the intense visceral realisation that becoming pregnant had set into motion a course of events to which I was now fully committed – whether I liked it or not. I *was* going to experience giving birth. I *was* going to experience the pain of the physical requirement of giving birth. I *was* going to experience all the consequences that naturally followed on from becoming pregnant. There is absolutely no backing out once that is set in motion.

PD: Gosh yes. I can see the potency of that feeling. But then, in these links, the baby is barely out of the womb, and is followed by the image of an old man carrying a body to the charnel ground, a corpse lying on the ground, and a vulture!

NN: *[Laughs]* Oh yes. There is no dwelling on the particulars of life.

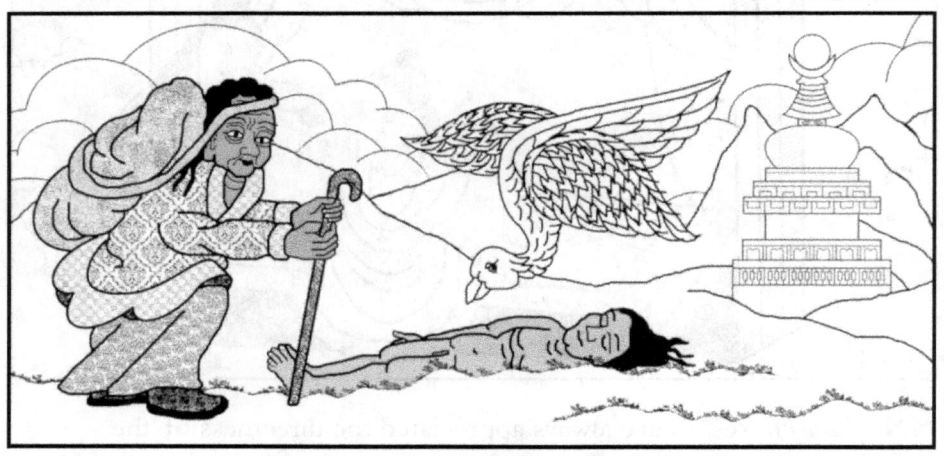

N'ö: Sickness, old age and death in a single concise image!

PD: So having looked quite quickly at the twelve images, are we going to go around the links again in more detail?

NN: Yes.

PD: Before we do that, could we just run through them again using the words that are traditionally associated with each link?

NN: Yes. Good idea.

PD: The blind person?

NN: Ignorance.

PD: The potter?

NN: Mental formations.

PD: The scampering monkey?

NN: Consciousness.

PD: The people in a boat?

NN: Name and form.

PD: The house?

NN: The six senses or the six sense sources.

PD: The lovers?

NN: Contact.

PD: The person with an arrow in their eye?

NN: Sensation.

PD: The person being served a drink?

NN: Craving.

PD: The fruit being gathered?

NN: Grasping or appropriation.

PD: The pregnant woman?

NN: Becoming.

PD: Is the next one just 'birth'?

NN: Yes.

PD: And I know the corpse-carrier represents death.

NN: Yes – old age and death. So now we are ready for a more in-depth discussion, starting again with ignorance.

PD: Could we look at your illustrations again as well, please, as we go through the links?

NN: Yes certainly. Here is the first one.

PD: Am I correct in thinking that the blind person is the main character in this link, rather than the child?

NN: Yes indeed. Sometimes the blind person is pictured alone. Sometimes they are shown walking clockwise, and sometimes—as here— walking anti-clockwise.

PD: So ignorance is the blind person… and it is the first link – but also the link that follows death if you look at it as an endless cycle. Is this the new rebirth's ignorance? Is it that nothing has been learned, they are reborn and have not escaped, and are stumbling along like a blind person?

NN: This sounds like you are still trying to make the links fit into a birth/death/rebirth scenario. This link is about the pattern of ignorance repeating, but not in the sense of a past and present life. Remember, this is *fundamental ignorance* – the ignorance that starts everything: the delusion of an inherent, or self-existing 'I'.

PD: Ignorance of reality causes the cycle of the links to start rolling?

NN: Yes.

PD: Do you think there is anything more to say about the symbolism of the person being blind?

NN: This could symbolise a number of things: blindness to the opportunity that was missed at the death of the last cycle to escape cyclic experience; blindness to the possibility of a new view, a new moment arising; blindness to fundamental ignorance; blindness to primordial awareness and beginningless enlightenment.

PD: Why is there a child?

NN: This is expressing that part of the nature of this blindness is not just an inability to see reality directly and clearly—that could be an open state—but that instead there is the mixing of old and new. The new state, moment, opportunity—the child—is closely connected to old, well-established patterns – the elderly person. There is a tendency to seek comfort and security in what is familiar.

PD: Is this what is meant by the wind of karmic patterning blowing beings back along old furrows.

N'ö: That sounds like something you read or heard somewhere.

PD: Yes it is.

NN: Could you rephrase it in your own words?

PD: Let me think… the empty space of *anything-could-happen* is experienced as too threatening, so I settle for turning back to what is familiar and feels safer instead?

NN: Good.

PD: Could there be a positive side to the blindness in this link – that blindness could enable you to avoid being snagged by sights which lure you back to a habitual furrow? Could blindness also represent emptiness?

NN: Blindness doesn't represent emptiness in this context, because this link is indicating the first movement toward form from the emptiness of death. Ignorance is the most subtle and insubstantial hint of form.

N'ö: The important message of this link is blind ignorance – that the mistaken view of an inherent identity is key at this point in the links of interdependent origination.

PD: Then we come to the potter – mental formations. Clay is an interesting substance. It is a sticky, plastic, amorphous mass that has no form of its own, but from it the potter can create an infinite variety of beautiful forms.

NN: What do you notice about the pots?

PD: Hmm… oh – they all seem to be about the same sort of size and shape.

NN: Good.

PD: Does this also refer to patterning being repeated?

NN: Yes.

PD: Something more has to happen to a pot before it becomes a useful vessel though – it has to be fired in a kiln.

NN: What happens if it is left alone?

PD: The clay will dry and eventually crack and crumble. Or alternatively, if it gets wet, it will dissolve back into a sticky mass again.

NN: It is the same with the nature of mind. It is an empty potential. It is natural for form to arise, and just as natural for form to dissolve back into emptiness. It is natural for Mind to be luminous and clear – if we learn how to leave it alone.

PD: A potter makes useful objects from the clay, so could this be an expression of the usefulness of the human realm? Most of the beings depicted in the links are human. Is it saying that something useful can be achieved in the human realm if we practise?

NN: No, that would be to stretch the meaning of the potter in the context of the links. Remember the words of the Sutra: *ignorance causes formations*. Mental formations are inevitable once there is fundamental ignorance. It is like setting a chemical reaction in motion. Once it has started, its momentum is inevitable.

PD: So patterning emerges from fundamental ignorance, which is why the pots all look the same?

N'ö: Yes. This is your 'wind of karmic patterning'. There is a tendency to repeat patterning.

PD: The image of a potter is fascinating… there is something tickling at the back of my mind… something about things would be alright if we didn't insist on baking our pots. We want to fix the form, and believe that we will discover certainty and security through fixing form.

NN: I like that analogy. Yes. Creating and re-creating the pot again and again… this is a symbol for the patterns of delusion we create or recreate over and over.

PD: But a clay pot isn't actually useful until it has been fired in a kiln. So this image could be confusing. Why don't we need to fire the pots that are created?

N'ö: That would be stretching it too far. Analogies are indications and cannot be taken too literally. It is the impermanent nature of the unfired clay that is relevant in this instance and the potter who can create form from the clay.

PD: Form could be open, clear, and vivid – but instead it's the same old pot again…?

NN: *[Laughs]* Yes. Something like that.

PD: So now, I think the next link is consciousness – represented by a monkey. It is the only one of the links—in this thangka—that uses an animal rather than a person or persons. Is it connected to the realms?

NN: No. The monkey is just used to illustrate the qualities of the mind – agile, lively, chaotic, wild. Sometimes a monkey reappears at the link showing grasping fruit – but—as you say— not in this thangka.

N'ö: There is also one link that is just a house…

PD: Ah yes… so not always people. I take your point.

NN: It is the restlessness of disembodied consciousness that is being expressed in this link. Mind is naturally clear and luminous, but because of the ignorance and patterning of the previous links, it is scampering over the building in an unruly manner. It is wild and undisciplined.

PD: Is being on a building an indication that it is not in its natural state?

NN: That is an interesting question. For this thangka, that is a pertinent interpretation.

N'ö: In many Wheel of Life thangkas the monkey is scampering in a tree, however – so it is the restless, lively nature of the monkey that is the primary point.

PD: The next link is *name and form*. I have heard it said that this refers to the skandhas?

NN: Yes, I have read that too in some commentaries. Three of the skandhas, however, are covered in other links. The five skandhas are form, feeling, perception, mental formations and consciousness. Mental formations and consciousness have already been mentioned. In this link, disembodied consciousness—which was depicted by the monkey—is now connected to manifest form. The boat is the body or form which enables perception and feeling.

PD: So these are represented by the four people in the boat?

N'ö: Some thangkas have only two or three people in the boat, so the number of people is not specifically significant.

PD: I think it's interesting that the people are travelling in a boat rather than it being a journey on horseback or some other means of transport. The boat moves in the water and contains its passengers. The water is the medium that enables movement. Travelling by boat has a particular sensory quality to it: the boat floats and glides and rocks with the water. It is not entirely separate from the water.

NN: That is well observed and captures the meaning of this link very well.

N'ö: This is the first link of manifest form. Mental formations and consciousness are embodied. Form—the boat—and the passengers—mental formations and consciousness—move, exist and are carried in the environment in which they manifest.

NN: I got very confused about one Wheel of Life painting I was examining… *[Laughs]* because there appeared to be a horse in the boat. I had not seen a horse in the boat in this link before. Eventually I was able to look closely enough to see that the horse was actually the boat's figurehead – it was a carving and part of the boat, not a passenger.

PD: *[Laughs]* How funny! So may I ask again why they appear to be monks in the boat?

NN: I don't know why the artist has painted them as ecclesiastics in this thangka. In my experience, this is not usual. It is more common for the passengers to be dressed in ordinary garb. So I suggest you ignore that they look like monks for the purpose of examining the meaning of the image.

PD: Okay. When you are in a boat there are objects to see, sensations to feel, the landscape changes as you travel. There may be a feeling about a destination. It is a rich image.

NN: Yes indeed. Even at this most subtle level of the beginning of form, there is the influence of fundamental ignorance.

N'ö: The open potential of creativity is constricted by fundamental ignorance: the naming of form as *me* or *mine*. So… *Ignorance causes formations. Formations cause consciousness. Consciousness causes name and form.* What does name and form cause?

PD: The six senses. An empty house with six windows.

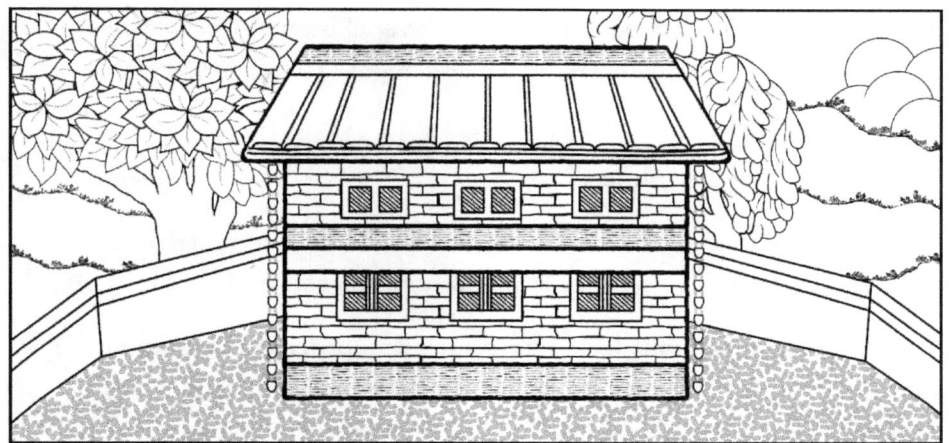

NN: Ngak'chang Rinpoche once described being human as: '… *viewing reality from within a pink sphere with six apertures – through which we: see, hear, smell, taste, touch, and ideate. We then take this to be all there is to reality. There could, of course, be other apertures of which we are unaware.*'

N'ö: Human beings see, hear, smell, taste, touch, and ideate within the limitations and with the capacities of human senses.

PD: If we are viewing the details of these images as symbolic, could this be a symbol of whatever form ignorance, formations, consciousness, and name and form have driven you towards, it will have the sensory characteristics that are caused by the previous links?

NN: Yes, that is correct.

PD: So this may not specifically refer to human senses – or not *only* refer to human senses?

NN: Yes. The cycle would follow the pattern of the links whatever the nature of form. A fly will see with compound insect eyes. A whale will have the capacity to hear whalesong many miles away. A dog will be able to recognise the time its owner is due to return home from work by sensing the diminishing potency of their scent in the house. A snake will examine the environment by tasting airborne flavours with its tongue. A cat will feel whatever is near it with sensitive whiskers. An eagle will be able to accurately calculate the speed and angle of its dive with eagle intelligence.

PD: Why is it an *empty* house?

NN: Because this is the *source* of the senses. We have not arrived at *contact* yet. There is no sensory reaction until the senses are stimulated.

PD: These last few links have felt to me like a process of grounding. The potter creates, but the clay could just dissolve back into mud. The monkey is free and wild, and so agile that it can roam and scamper all over its environment. The boat is carried by the currents in the river. The people in the boat can flow with those currents and travel in the boat. But then, there is the house. It is grounded, static, empty. It even has a wall around it.

NN: This is again a useful observation. The illusory 'I' wants to feel solid, secure, and grounded in a nice house with a wall round it. It wants to feel it has an identity that will be permanent and continue.

N'ö: Consciousness is setting up home to support its belief in a self-existing 'I'.

NN: Yes – a nice chic little house with a protective wall.

PD: But the house exists in an environment. There are going to be neighbours, and birds and animals. The source of the senses inevitably makes contact with phenomena.

NN: Yes, and this is illustrated by the next link – the lovers. In other thangkas this is depicted as a less fully-formed relationship. It might be a couple embracing, or enjoying their first kiss.

PD: But this link *is* about relationship – the relationship between the senses and that which the senses encounter?

NN: Yes.

N'ö: The house makes contact with external phenomena via its six windows: seeing, hearing, tasting, smelling, touching, and ideating.

NN: The image representing contact always concerns relationship. It is also an image which suggests that contact is pleasurable. Fundamentally being embodied is a source of enjoyment, appreciation, and love. If there was direct experience and appreciation, pleasure could continue unbounded.

PD: Right… I hear that and understand it… but the next link seems to contradict this. Contact is followed by the picture of a person with an arrow in their eye! Ouch! Why is sensation portrayed as so painful?

NN: It is more an expression of intensity – of the rawness of direct contact before patterning clicks in and there is classification and analysis.

N'ö: The arrow in the eye is a dynamic image. It is not pulling any punches. The eye is a sensitive organ and the idea of getting penetrated in the eye by a sharp arrow is intense. We smart and suffer from the tiniest fleck in the eye, so the person looking at this image will understand that this is sharp and intense.

NN: The first experience of sensation arising from contact is extraordinarily intense. Naked direct sensation is single-pointed.

PD: So are you saying that sensation *should* have this intensity?

NN: Yes indeed. We lose the directness and immediacy of whatever the senses perceive because of ignorance, patterned formations, consciousness, name and form.

N'ö: Experience is filtered through patterning rather than being direct.

NN: It is not experienced simply as *sensation*. It is experienced as **my** *sensation* – which creates an extra requirement of the sensation: of having to go through the filter of questioning whether it is good for me or bad for me. The *good for me or bad for me* filter is a concept based on ignorance that believes in a self-existing 'I'.

N'ö: Pleasure and pain are both sensations. It is concept that polarises them as desirable and undesirable.

PD: Right. So is the next image looking at the relationship with that intensity? The intensity is so vivid that it is intoxicating. We want more.

NN: Yes, that's correct. The image describes craving. A person is being served an alcoholic drink.

PD: Is this as simple as 'sensation is intoxicating'?

NN: Yes. Why not? These images are intended to be direct and understandable. Remember that the Wheel of Life is on the *outside* of the lhakhang so that everyone can read it and gain an understanding. These images are not intended to only be decipherable by erudite intellectuals. The images are intended to explain themselves.

N'ö: This image —*[Laughs]*—always reminds me of a scene in a Star Trek film.

PD: Oh really? Do please say more.

NN: I think I know the scene you are thinking of…

N'ö: It concerns the character Data, who is an android and thus far has been unable to experience sensation or emotion. He has just installed an 'emotion chip' which will enable him to sensate for the first time. He goes, with a comrade, to 10-Forward—the starship's recreation room—and requests an alcoholic beverage. He drinks it and pulls a face. The bartender says, '*Well, it looks like he hates it.*' Data says excitedly, '*Yes. That is it. I hate this!*' He drinks the rest of the beverage and exclaims, '*Oh, yes! I hate this! It is revolting!*' He is highly animated by the experience. The bartender, recognising the exhilaration of the intensity of the new experience, asks, '*More?*' and Data replies with a big grin, '*Please!*'

PD: Ha, ha – yes! I can see how he found the newness and intensity of that first sensory experience so exciting. He wants to repeat it even though it is unpleasant. You can see this excitement about a new experience in children.

NN: Yes, well Data is one of those science fiction characters who is childlike with regard to everyday experiences – it's a science fiction trope.

PD: So the intensity leads to a craving for more, to perpetuate the intensity of contact and sensation?

NN: Yes, but unfortunately reference to *me* becomes the primary factor, rather than contact and sensation that is naked, open, and fresh.

N'ö: There is the paradox of the desire for the intensity of new, fresh and open contact, whilst at the same time wanting to check the safety of contact via the *is it good for me* or *bad for me* filter. It becomes impossible to simply allow the flow of sensation to unfold.

PD: So this is like becoming an addict – continually craving for a repetition of what has just been experienced rather than allowing that experience to die—end—and embracing whatever the next experience may be.

N'ö: Yes.

NN: Because there is the desire to repeat experience that is known, rather than being open to whatever the new experience might be – however much is drunk, the craving is never fully satisfied. You drink and drink until you are exhausted and give up, or until the whisky runs out.

PD: Is the fear that the whisky will run out the primary cause of grasping?

NN: It is more the *fear* of direct experience, entwined with the *desire* for direct experience. Interpreting present experience through past experience feels safer than direct experience. This is duality. Grasping at form and denying the emptiness of change and movement.

N'ö: Direct experience is unknowable – it will always be new and fresh. It is empty until tasted.

NN: But that emptiness is frightening to the self that wants to be in control. *Not knowing* is threatening.

N'ö: So the self that wants to be in control settles for interpreted experience rather than direct experience as the safer option, but this is inevitably unsatisfying.

PD: When you look at it, it seems really foolish. Contact and sensation will never cease. There is no reason to doubt that it will continue. Yet the wish to control experience spoils it.

NN: Fundamental ignorance fears *that which is as yet unknown*, because it is emptiness. To embrace that emptiness would be to let go of **me**. So *that which has already been experienced and did not seem to threaten* **me** is regarded as more desirable.

PD: It does look a bit daft when you analyse it. The next, *currently-unknown experience* could be fabulous as well – or even more fabulous.

N'ö: Yes. Protecting the illusory 'I' creates an insistence on going for what is familiar. Experience will inevitably continue in the way a river flows. All that has to be done is to stay in that boat and enjoy it!

PD: But instead a house is built by the river to watch it, rather than being there in the flow of it. The house feels safer and more secure. The spectator in the house, both craves and fears the intensity of contact and sensation.

NN: Yes indeed. Fundamental ignorance—the illusory 'I'—creates the idea of *owning* and controlling experience rather than just flowing with it.

PD: The next link is *grasping* – a person gathering fruit.

NN: It is often portrayed as a monkey grasping a piece of fruit in a tree, but it isn't particularly significant whether it is a monkey or a person. The baskets of fruit around the gatherer are worth mentioning. Not only does craving grasp at the fruit, it wants to accumulate and have a whole store of it.

PD: So this is about classifying again rather than direct experience?

NN: Indeed. It feels more secure to have a whole store of already classified and gathered fruit, than embracing new and fresh perceptual experience.

PD: Looking at these last few links, they all seem connected to patterning. Are these all about making pots? Are they about making the same pots over and over again?

NN: Yes. Old patterns are continued and added to. Even new experiences are checked out according to what has already happened.

PD: So could it be said that the methods of Dharma—whatever the vehicle of practice—are about learning to make a new sort of pot, as indicated by the teacher?

NN: *[Laughs]* That is a useful way of looking at it.

PD: And we have to practise making the new sort of pot a lot, so that it becomes second nature?

NN: Oh yes.

N'ö: But ultimately the new type of pot—the method or path of practice—has to be let go of as well. Then creation becomes unconditioned and spontaneous.

PD: So the potter has to stop using the pattern in their mind and let whatever arises arise…

NN: … and experience that directly and immediately without comparing it to the old pattern of pot.

PD: Alright… and now there is the link *becoming* which is followed by *birth*. What is becoming and being born?

NN: *Becoming* is the result of the previous links. Each link is the cause of the next one, and the result of contact, sensation, craving, and grasping is that a particular form becomes fully manifest.

PD: The same old pot or a new pot?

NN: The pots refer more to the patterning of the mind. Here the links are moving into energetic and physical manifestation.

PD: So is this the point of actual birth?

NN: Yes.

PD: As the next level of the Wheel—moving in towards the hub—depicts the six realms of existence, I assume that birth is occurring in one of those realms?

NN: Yes.

PD: So this is a rebirth. Yet you said earlier that from the perspective of Vajrayana, the Wheel of Life is not interpreted as describing actual physical rebirth?

NN: Correct.

PD: Yet here is a birth, and a realm where rebirth is taking place.

NN: Yes, but what is being incarnated?

PD: A being is incarnating…

NN: Yes, that is true. But what is the nature of the incarnation?

PD: A being in one of the six realms?

NN: Yes… and how long does that incarnation manifest?

PD: I don't know. Chögyam Trungpa Rinpoche described the realms as mind-states rather than as physical realms for rebirth. Is that what is indicated here?

N'ö: Yes. Also the XIVth Dala'i Lama stated as far back as the 1980s, that the six realms were perceptual states and not actual places.

NN: Chögyam Trungpa Rinpoche also said that the skandhas arise in a 500th of a second.

PD: Ah – so this is why you are asking about the length of an incarnation. It depends on the speed of change. What is the speed of the turning of the Wheel?

NN: The Wheel of Life turns at the speed of Mind. We are travelling at the speed of Mind. Every 500th of a second we take rebirth in a realm.

PD: So it *is* a story of a lifetime, but the *lifetime* lasts a fraction of a second?

NN: This is the view of the cycle of the interdependent links from the perspective of Vajrayana. This view removes the need to try and make life experience fit the images. It is a logical and workable view that is easy to understand and makes sense of the images.

PD: It does seem a straightforward way of looking at them. Form arises —over several links—manifests, abides and dissolves. In fact—just to complete the links—the final image is of an old man carrying a corpse and the charnel ground is the dissolution: old age, sickness and death.

N'ö: Absolutely. The only possible outcome of birth is death. Birth of form leads to the dissolution of form, and finally the death of that form. Death and impermanence are a vital point in all the Buddhist teachings.

NN: This is continual, Mind moment by Mind moment.

N'ö: All the links occur in the arising of that Mind moment. Then it abides, dissolves, and ends.

PD: That clearly makes sense of why nothing really happens—in terms of the links—between birth and death. There are no intermediary links there because it is not describing a whole lifetime – human or otherwise. It is describing a Mind moment.

NN: From fundamental ignorance of the nature of reality, the illusion of an inherent self arises. From this ignorance patterning which supports the illusion of an inherent self manifests: mental formations, consciousness, and the processes of self-identification through name and form, and the sources of the senses. Then there is engagement with experience through contact and sensation, which leads to craving and grasping. This concretises self-identification and a particular style—or rebirth—comes into being and is born.

N'ö: It is all based on the first link, fundamental ignorance. This fundamental wrong belief in a self-existing 'I' creates duality and dissatisfaction. Rebirth in a realm where dissatisfaction is experienced is inevitable whilst there is fundamental ignorance.

NN: The links describe samsara or 'khorwa – cyclic existence: the flow from emptiness into form and back to emptiness is a trap of dissatisfaction because of fundamental ignorance.

N'ö: If realisation arises with regard to the fundamental view of ignorance—that there is *not* a self-existing 'I'—this will cut patterning. The experience of form arising from emptiness and dissolving back into emptiness could be a cycle of everlasting direct experience and infinite joy.

PD: So the message of the Wheel is that we create whatever becomes and is born, and it is fundamental ignorance that makes that an experience of samsara rather than nirvana?

NN: Oh most certainly. There is the chaos of circumstances occurring over which we have no control, but we are always responsible for our relationship with, and response to, those circumstances. We are not victims. We actively create the type of life we end up living, through perception and response. We create our own Wheel of Life – our own experience of the circumstances.

PD: So unless patterning is actively undermined through spiritual practice, once you arrive at *becoming*, you are locked into the form of life you have created through the previous links.

NN: For that Mind-moment.

PD: Oh yes, of course. There is always the opportunity of the next Mind-moment.

N'ö: This is the pertinent message of the Wheel of Life. There is always a choice in how you respond to experience.

NN: A practitioner cannot control circumstances, and may have limited control of patterning until capacity develops, but you can always control response. Response is the great responsibility of a practitioner.

N'ö: Indeed. Buddhist practice—especially silent sitting—enables a practitioner to develop the spaciousness to become aware of response, even when there is little control over patterning.

PD: So could there be a different Wheel of Life? A Wheel where there is no fundamental ignorance at the top so that everything unfolds and moves round with wisdom, compassion and selflessness?

NN: Yes. If there is clarity instead of blindness, then the being that arises in the moment can enjoy and play with being embodied. Perception could be a magical appreciative dance with phenomena.

PD: So as form always arises, abides and dissolves, how can we make this a cycle of awakening rather than delusion?

NN: Through openness and appreciation. Keep your windows open and let phenomena connect. Experience directly, appreciating everything, and understand that external phenomena—whatever is contacted and sensed—is perfect exactly as it is.

PD: Is each moment governed by view, perception and response?

NN: Yes, and we have to be aware of where we are setting up house in each moment. This is what we will look at in the next session about the realms. We must ask ourselves moment-by-moment: *am I in the human realm in this moment, or in a less useful realm in terms of awakening?*

PD: So the links can be understood as spontaneously arising in each Mind-moment? They are all spontaneously present in the moment – and then the next, and the next, and the next…?

NN: Absolutely. Yes – being able to be present and aware at each point in the links, will dissolve duality and the chain of causality.

PD: But realisation does not end life, so what would that mean to an incarnate being?

NN: Form would continue until it dissolved—in terms of a lifespan—but the relationship with each mind-moment would be realisation—the nonduality of emptiness and form—rather than delusion – the grasping and fixation of form. Realisation would mean that to continue with an incarnate form, and taking rebirth again, becomes a choice, an act of compassion – rather than the result of conditioned causality. Every link is a choice.

N'ö: This has been quite a long session. It is time for a break now, and we must prepare dinner.

PD: Yes I agree… but… what Ngakma-la just said has stirred something quite emotional in me.

NN: Oh? Would you like to say more?

PD: The great teachers who have gained realisation of nonduality come back to us again and again. They choose to be here for our benefit. That is so extraordinary and moving. It has inspired a deeper feeling of devotion than I have ever experienced before.

NN: *[Smiling and speaking quietly.]* You have understood very clearly.

The Six Realms

5 – The Six Realms

It is evening, and the last session of the day examining the Wheel of Life.

PD: The six realms do not seem to be in fixed positions on the Wheel – apart from the hell realm which is always at the bottom and the god realm which is always at the top.

NN: Yes that is true. The other four realms can be found on either side. Sometimes the human and animal realm are next to each other, and sometimes the hungry ghost realm is next to the human realm. One thing that always seems to be assured is that the three lower realms—hells, hungry ghost and animal—are at the bottom; and the three higher realms—human, demi-god and god—are at the top.

PD: Yes. I see. Also when the realms are discussed, sometimes the order changes there as well.

N'ö: The order of the realms depends on the perspective of the discussion. If they are being discussed in terms of speed of perception and response, the order will be: hell, hungry ghost, animal, human, demi-god and god realms.

NN: The speed of perception and response in the hell realm is so fast that it seems instantaneous. Then moving up through the realms it becomes slower, until in the god realm, perception and response is so slow that life seems eternal.

N'ö: If the realms are being discussed in terms of value or hindrance with regard to Buddhist practice and liberation, then they will be examined in the order of: hell, hungry ghost, animal, god, demi-god and finally the human realm.

PD: Oh I see. What order shall we discuss them in?

NN: What would you prefer?

PD: I think in terms of usefulness for practice.

NN: Good choice. That would be my preference as well. We start with the hell realm anyway. Would you like to see my illustrations again, taken from the thangka?

PD: Yes please. I found those really helpful. So shall I say something about the hell realm?

NN: Please do.

PD: In the thangka the beings in the hell realm are clearly shown to be having a most unpleasant existence. There is burning and boiling; there is iciness and freezing. Some beings are being stabbed with various pointed objects, and some seem to be experiencing painful scenarios reminiscent of medieval torture, such as being stretched on a rack. There are also strange demon-like beings and blue beings with animal heads…

NN: My illustrations show just a small part of the hell realm section in the thangka, as it is quite a large image. I have illustrated just the two rectangular details divided into eight types of hot hell and eight types of cold hell.

N'ö: Ngak'chang Rinpoche describes hell beings as: *'Perditional pandemoniacs, sado-masochistic victims of vicious self-inflicted torture who inhabit an emotive slaughterhouse where the slaughterers are emotionally slaughtered as they slaughter – by their own means of psychiatric slaughtering.'*

PD: Phew!

NN: This is the fastest realm. Perception, response, and suffering are so fast as to be experienced as simultaneous. Threat is perceived, and an aggressive self-protective response arises. The pain of being both the perpetrator and the victim of anger and aggression is continuous. The hells are characterised by a wish to destroy the object of fear.

PD: So the cycle that is being repeated is trying to make samsara work through aggression.

NN: Yes. The perception of threat and the aggressive defence is so fast that it appears automatic and therefore normal.

PD: I have occasionally experienced that you cannot reason with angry people. They perceive kindness and reason as aggression.

NN: Quite. Only exhaustion can create a gap in this scenario. Satisfaction is found through the destruction of the object of threat, but the very act of destruction creates fear of the next threat.

PD: And the feeling of being threatened can arise from pretty much anything, I think?

NN: Yes – if you dress differently to me, or you have a different sexual orientation, or you follow a different religion, or you have different likes and dislikes, or you are too short or too tall, you are too fat or too thin, your skin is the wrong colour… and so on.

PD: So basically difference is to be feared. It is a threat.

N'ö: Yes. Wherever I see a difference to my definition of self it is perceived as a threat, and—ultimately—I have to destroy that threat. This is an instantaneous knee-jerk reaction: see it / hate it / destroy it… see it / hate it / destroy it… see it / hate it / destroy it… in perpetuum.

PD: Hate is not that common in ordinary life though, don't you think?

NN: It is a spectrum, a range. The snide comment that you say to yourself that no one will ever know about or hear, is one end of the spectrum, and murder is at the other end – but each are part of the path of hatred and the wish to destroy whatever is perceived as challenging and threatening.

PD: The unvoiced snide comment doesn't hurt anyone or destroy anything though.

NN: Doesn't it? Are you sure about that?

PD: Well I suppose it hurts yourself, because it creates a negative pattern in relation to that person.

NN: Exactly. And it destroys the possibility of appreciation. It destroys the possibility of a pleasant encounter.

PD: I remember one time playing the game of 'Rebirth' with you after a retreat and there were descriptions of several types of hell in the explanatory book that accompanies the board game.

N'ö: Yes. Let's run through some of those. The cold hells describe the unpleasantness of being intolerably cold – from shivering, chattering teeth, and cracking skin to becoming completely frozen. If completely frozen, there is no capacity to move the mouth and victims can only groan. The cold hells where the skin splits are named in terms of lotus petals. Where the flesh is like a blue lotus, it splits into six petals. Where the flesh is like a red lotus, it splits into ten petals. There is another cold hell where the flesh splits like a thousand-petalled lotus.

PD: Ah… So those are the marks on the bodies of the beings in the eight-section cold hell illustration?

NN: Yes.

PD: Oh heck. I sometimes get a split in the skin on my thumb in severe cold weather and it is extremely painful. Imagine having your flesh splitting in that way all over your body!

NN: Indeed. The hot hells are also no picnic. In reviving hell you are continually killed and revived to be killed again. In black rope hell beings are bound with black cords and then sliced along the line marks left by the cords. In crushing hell, beings are crushed between mountains, revived and crushed again.

PD: No fun at all!

NN: The one that particularly catches my imagination is the hell of sharp leaves. Here you are tempted to climb a tree by the alluring phantom of your lover waiting for you at the top. The hot sharp leaves face downwards as you climb the tree, slicing and burning your body. When you get to the top, your lover then appears on the ground so you have to climb back down – but the leaves cruelly reverse direction and slice and burn your body again as you descend.

PD: That is very graphic.

N'ö: In the howling hells your mouth is filled with molten copper. The hot and very hot hells have torture by molten bronze and piercing with sharp weapons. Interminable hell is a prison of flame and molten metal. Vajra hell is the worst of the hell realms, reserved for vow-breakers, and is characterised by paranoia.

PD: Oh my! But these are not real places, are they?

NN: They are not. It is central to our Lineage to view the realms as states of mind rather than actual physical locations for rebirth.

PD: I believe Chögyam Trungpa Rinpoche was the first person to talk about the realms in that way.

N'ö: Yes, and—as we said earlier—the XIVth Dala'i Lama also does not regard the realms as actually existent places to be physically reborn.

PD: The speed of the hell realms feels quite claustrophobic – being locked into that view.

NN: Yes, the fast speed of hell realm perception and response *is* claustrophobic, allowing no space for an alternative view to arise. If you find yourself in this realm, every look, word, and action of another person, and every situation that arises, is perceived as threatening and immediately responded to with aggressive self-protection.

PD: So everyone will be viewed as an enemy or potential enemy – even those who try to be kind to you.

NN: Exactly. Because of your own aggression you expect everything in your environment to be as aggressive as you are, and so you constantly fear attack. The attack strategy will either be emotionally hot or emotionally cold – raging, rampant, ruthless, barbaric, brutal, bloodthirsty, violent, vicious, vindictive, callous, cruel, cold-blooded, murderous, malevolent, mean…

PD: I can see how some of these descriptions of the hells could describe ordinary circumstances – but presented in an extreme form. For example with the black rope hell, if you experience bad circumstances, that can leave a sort of mark – there is a memory physically, emotionally and mentally. If you hold onto those marks and interpret new situations with reference to that memory, then it is just like you keep cutting yourself on the mark that is left. You expect the situation to hurt like it did before, and so you in fact recreate it through that expectation and perpetuate the pattern of pain and emotional turmoil.

NN: Yes, indeed. It is good to be able to see this. You cut yourself and others along the marks of referentiality. You never allow the marks to disappear but continually add to the lattice of referentiality. It is extremely valuable to recognise how these states can refer to ordinary life circumstances.

N'ö: This is in fact more valuable, and potent, than viewing these states as something to be feared in a future life, because it is so immediate and could happen at any moment.

PD: Reviving hell is like when you keep actively reviving some strong emotion around a past hurt or grievance, because the intensity of the pain of feeling it again and again is somehow easier to bear than letting it go.

NN: Oh yes – burning and boiling, anger and aggression, fear and pain. They are intense, but somehow the uncomfortable familiarity of the pain feels more secure than the uncomfortable unknowing emptiness of letting them go.

PD: So the speed and claustrophobia of the hell realms makes it very difficult to experience any gap?

NN: Yes. Stimulus and reaction are practically simultaneous. When one's whole experience is fear of being attacked, it is quite intelligent to regard attacking first as a means of safety. The problem is that it is a closed spiral that tightens and becomes more and more intense. Ultimately the threat has to be annihilated, totally destroyed.

PD: So what hope is there of escaping a hellish state of mind if you get stuck there?

N'ö: The pattern of intensity has to cease for escape to be possible, and this can happen through exhaustion or a glimpse of an alternative view. Eventually the speed and repetition of the pattern of hellish intensity leads to exhaustion and that creates a little gap. If you can embrace that gap then you may suddenly find yourself in a different realm.

NN: If you think of that point of exhaustion as *death* in the twelve links, the new cycle has a chance of revolving round to *becoming* and *birth* and leading into a different realm.

PD: Wow. Just talking about the hell realms feels quite claustrophobic and desperate.

NN: Yes, but Buddhism never gives up on anyone. Every state of confusion is regarded as workable. In Vajrayana every state of confusion is a basis for transformation.

N'ö: Any and every experiential existence can be experienced as hellish or ecstatic – it is the Mind and view that creates the difference. What matters is how the teachings on the realms impact us in terms of practice.

NN: When I first heard these teachings I found them to be a deterrent to practice rather than an encouragement.

PD: Oh really, why was that?

NN: I felt that if a moment of anger could result in being condemned to a hell realm rebirth, then I'd already blown it for this life anyway, so what was the point in practice? It also felt too much like a threat: *be good or else* – a return to a view of sin, judgement and condemnation which was a spiritual approach I had rejected.

PD: How did you come to find it a useful teaching?

NN: By becoming a student of Ngak'chang Rinpoche and Khandro Déchen; by reading Chögyam Trungpa Rinpoche's books; by learning about the Dzogchen view of beginningless enlightenment rather than original sin; and through common sense. The Buddhist teachings emphasise basic goodness and intention. Continuing good-hearted intention is clearly beyond measure in its power and impact on the mindstream. This reality can be discovered experientially through practice.

PD: Are the demons engaged in the torture our own demonic mindstates?

N'ö: Yes absolutely. No one is doing this to you. If you are trapped in the hell realm, you are doing it to yourself. If the slightest possibility arises of seeing that the demon that is hurting you is your own reaction to threat, then there is space, and movement and change become possible.

PD: The chain of claustrophobic repetition is broken.

NN: Exactly.

PD: I can see how that cycle can be created. Anticipating a bad situation with someone you don't get on with or don't like for some reason, influences how you behave with them. You might be short with them, and misinterpret innocent—or even friendly—looks and comments as unfriendly. This causes you to be more self-protective… hang on a minute… I seem to be describing the links! Anticipation is ignorance, which leads to mental formations… and all the following links are based in that anticipation of it being bad – and suddenly you are in the hell realm in that moment.

NN: Yes. That is it. The outer ring of the twelve links demonstrates how you are born into any of these six realms.

PD: Viewing this teaching as describing continually arising rebirths, moment by moment, is extremely powerful.

NN: I agree.

PD: So this repeats for all the realms. The point of ignorance, deluded perception, sets the whole process into action?

NN: Yes. You could say that this section of the wheel gives all the details about *a life* that seem to be missing in the twelve interdependent links.

PD: Of course. It isn't a series of teachings, section by section, it is the same teaching throughout, examined in different ways in each ring.

N'ö: Indeed. It is a very common method in Buddhist teaching – to take a subject apart and look at it piece by piece, whilst understanding that the subject is actually inseparable.

PD: Could you give an example?

N'ö: How about the spheres of being: Nirmanakaya, Sambhogakaya and Dharmakaya? These can be understood as body, speech and mind; form, energy and emptiness – and they are inseparable. It is perfectly reasonable and helpful however, to look at them separately in order to help understand how they are inseparable.

PD: Yes. Thank you. That's very helpful. So shall we look at the next realm of possible rebirth in the order we have adopted: the hungry ghosts?

NN: Please go on.

PD: These are strange looking creatures. They are almost like human beings but seem to have huge abdomens and tiny thin necks. They are naked and look unhappy, but they do not seem to be being tormented in the way the hell realm beings are clearly suffering.

NN: Good.

PD: There is a single blue demon in the image next to a basket of fruit. There is also a lot of fire in this realm, but it looks as though they are trying to eat it or something. The environment looks quite normal and not particularly uncomfortable.

N'ö: This is what Ngak'chang Rinpoche says about this realm. He describes the beings as: *'tormented inadequates – insatiable, unquenchable, self-defeating, emaciated, gluttonous, malnourished, rapacious voracipaths who inhabit the McDonald's of Mordor.'*

PD: Oh yes. So a hungry ghost is always hungry but cannot relate to wholesome food as nutrition?

NN: That's right. They simply cannot see it as food. Whatever they *do* try to eat turns to poison or fire. Even if they are told that what they are being given is wholesome, they cannot see it that way.

PD: In the tshogs'khorlo feast an offering is put outside for the hungry ghosts. We have to scrunch it up and put it in an old or dirty bowl and leave it somewhere unsavoury, like by the outside toilet.

NN: Yes. This is the only way they can see it as food. If it were presented beautifully in a clean bowl on a lovely cloth, it would not look like something they could eat.

PD: I guess it is scrunched up, because with their thin necks they can only swallow smushed up food.

N'ö: You could look at it like that as well. The food has to be presented in a manner that makes sense to the mindstate of the hungry ghost.

PD: So, thinking about this as a mindstate, would this be when someone is never satisfied with any help you give them, and never happy even when things are going well.

NN: Yes.

PD: I can think of a few people who seem to always spoil things somehow – like they have to complain about a tiny detail when you are out for a meal with them; or you come out of the cinema feeling elated or moved by the film you have watched and they destroy the magic of it by intellectual analysis.

NN: Exactly. Such responses can really deflate the joy of a situation. But it is more useful to see the pattern in yourself. Seeing a pattern in others may enable you to help them, but there is the danger of it preventing you seeing it in yourself.

PD: I understand what you are saying. Hmm… let me think… Sometimes my partner has kindly finished a household chore so that I don't have to, and I can't stop myself criticising how it was done and feeling that I would have made a better job of it myself – that sort of thing. Spoiling something that was wholesome and kind.

NN: Good example! *[Laughs.]*

PD: Again, this is not a place that really exists?

NN: No – and that doesn't matter in terms of understanding the message of the teaching.

PD: But we do put out the hungry ghost bowl in the tsog feast…

N'ö: Ngak'chang Rinpoche has said that the yidag offering could simply be described as *theatre*. He said: '*It's a symbolic act. Enacting the yidag profferment is an effort – and that effort supports bodhicitta.*'

NN: What is important is the principle of being open to the possibility of being able to help, and—in the context of the Wheel of Life—the recognition of the pattern of that mindstate.

PD: So it is that pattern of: *I eat it and it burns me. I eat, but am immediately hungry again.*

NN: Yes.

PD: Why are there baskets of fruit?

NN: The fruit is the wholesome food to which they are unable to relate. The point of this is that this food is there in their realm, but they do not see it as food. They cannot access and benefit from it. So the demon—the hungry ghost's own perception—drives them away from the fruit.

PD: Okay. I think we have finished with that realm. The next realm is more familiar: the animal realm. This seems quite straightforward. There are recognisable animals from our own world and some that look more mythological. They are in a natural landscape and are just… well… they are just being animals.

N'ö: Ngak'chang Rinpoche calls the beings of this realm: '*primitive instinctualists: mono-linear, blinkered, myopic, prejudiced, bigoted, intolerant, herd-mentality, heterophobic belligerents whose peak of happiness is to inhabit a slough of moronic mediocrity.*'

5 – *The Six Realms*

PD: *[Laughs]* Oh dear! This seems to relate to having an opinion or view that is locked into a lack of wisdom or insight – of limiting the scope of one's life in order to try to control it.

NN: That is certainly an aspect. Animal realm beings are locked into a narrow view that is never questioned, but stuck to rigidly. Your view is your territory. How things are, is how things should be, and how things will always be. You just have to get on with it.

PD: So is it bad to have opinions and preferences?

NN: No. This is not to say that opinions and preferences are inherently bad. It is fine to have an opinion or a preference. The problem is when that becomes a reason to stop being open – when it becomes a reference point to support an identity. Remember fundamental ignorance – the delusion of an inherent, self-existing 'I'. The animal realm uses opinions to support the structure of ignorance.

N'ö: Khandro Dechen once said to me: *'It is not a problem to have opinions, as long as one realises they are subjective – and can run contrary to the subjectivity of others. Everyone's subjectivity is equally valid or equally invalid.'*

PD: So in the animal realm, life becomes some sort of furrow, just following the familiar routine and pattern. If it is relatively comfortable it is cherished and never challenged.

NN: That's right. If someone offers a new, alternative viewpoint you refuse to even look at it. You become disgruntled if your familiar routine is disrupted.

PD: I think there was also something about herd mentality in this realm?

NN: Yes. Although you are fundamentally kind, you will join in the unpleasantness directed at another group of people, because it feels safer to remain in the shared view of your own group. To confront or question the unpleasantness of your group would be to question the herd mentality.

N'ö: You are blinkered, locked into the shafts of your personal mindset, pulling your security-cart full of habits, opinions, prejudices and limitations. You do not look up, but plough on in a straight line, ignoring or trampling new possibilities and opportunities as you trudge along.

NN: New experiences and views are avoided in favour of the security of trudging along the same old furrow.

PD: And it may be that someone else decided on the furrow in the first place.

N'ö: Yes. Mindlessly following fashion would be an example of this. You do not even *look* at whether you actually like the current fashion, you adopt it because it is what everyone else is doing. Conforming is safety.

PD: Some people believe that animals are kinder, more intelligent, and more aware than human beings…

NN: That could certainly be true for individual animals who are perhaps able to step out of the mindset of their realm, despite having the physical appearance of an animal realm being. It is the principle of the realm that is being addressed here.

PD: So perhaps the kinder or more aware animal is actually in the human realm?

NN: Yes. And the opinionated, belligerent human is actually in the animal realm. The animal *realm* is where behaviour is patterned and instinctive. A badger always lives in a sett. A nesting bird always builds a nest. Animals have characteristics of their species which do not generally change.

N'ö: Badgers do not build dams to live in – that is what beavers do. British bats do not hunt during the day. It is this quality of being locked into the pattern of your species that is being used to characterise the animal realm mindset, rather than making a value judgement about actual or individual animals.

PD: Yes. I can see that. I find that realm quite easy to understand.

NN: Yes. Good. Now in the order we are taking these realms—of usefulness to practice—we jump to the god realm next.

PD: Could another way of explaining this order—hell, hungry ghost, animal, god, demi-god and human—be the likelihood of escape from the cycle of rebirth?

NN: Yes it could. There is a greater chance of seeing the pattern of the cycle and questioning it in the human realm than in any of the others. All the others are either too fast to have a chance to look; too dull for a question to arise; or too close to seeming to make samsara work to give up on that effort.

PD: This would be true even if you are not a practitioner?

NN: Yes… but… as you will see when we discuss the human realm, it is the importance of dwelling in the *Precious Human* realm that is the point in this teaching.

PD: But that is not reserved only for Buddhists?

NN: Oh, I see what you are asking. No. This is a Buddhist teaching so it emphasises that Buddhism is the best practice. But no, the qualities of the human realm are always available to anyone and everyone. But shall we return to the god realm?

PD: Yes. Let's. Why is this the next in the sequence in terms of being able to engage in practice?

N'ö: Ngak'chang Rinpoche describes the gods as: '*smug, terminally phlegmatic, self-assured, self-satisfied, languidly-imperious narcissists who inhabit a dream-world so perfect that it is devoid of meaning.*'

PD: Ah… so there is no stimulus to change or explore?

NN: That's right. The god realm is locked into its own existence and limited, similarly to the animal realm, but here it is the limitation of perfection that offers no impetus to change. They believe they have made samsara work, or that they are realised.

PD: So they are having such a wonderful life that there is no sense of dissatisfaction – it does not occur to them that they need to look at anything.

NN: That's correct. They are disconnected from any reality other than their own dreamlike perfection. The god realm is like holding a breath – eventually you have to breathe again. It is a static state. You don't do anything useful for yourself or for others. You just rest in an impenetrable state of perfection.

PD: You are so wealthy that it is impossible to spend your riches fast enough to reduce the vastness of your fortune…

N'ö: … and you are oblivious to the underpaid workers who support the edifice of your perfection.

PD: The thangka does not seem to have as much detail as the other realms in terms of the quality of the realm. The gods seem to live in the clouds on top of a great tree, and to be defending themselves from the attackers on the ground. In fact these two realms do not seem to be separate in the same way as the others.

NN: Yes. In some traditions they are described as the five realms of being, with the god and demi-god realms being considered a single realm.

PD: The fact that the gods are under attack and defending themselves seems to be a contradiction to the perfection of their existence.

NN: That's a good point, but they are pretty unassailable in their lofty heaven. The attackers cannot really get at them. In this thangka it does look like a war is going on. In others, the gods seem pretty unaware of the demi-gods firing arrows at them and are simply going about their godly business.

PD: I believe the gods are said to have extremely long and protracted lives?

NN: Correct. They do not need to work to sustain themselves. Everything they need or desire simply appears for their enjoyment. However, if they were to suffer an injury, they could die. They are not immortal. So perhaps this is why they defend their realm.

PD: So the danger here is that when my life is going well, I am healthy and happy, and everything seems lovely… I may not bother to engage in practice. I might relax into the pleasure of comfortable circumstances and believe I have achieved satisfaction.

N'ö: Indeed. The gods may even believe they are realised and awakened. They are oblivious to the unreality of their existence and to the existence of others.

PD: Isn't this really where we all want to live though?

NN: *[Laughs]* Do go on.

PD: Isn't it what we all dream of: not having to work but always having what you need... perfect health... beauty and pleasantness...

NN: Apply your human capacity to examine that.

PD: Hmm... it would be like always being on holiday in a perfect hotel in a perfect setting... I guess I wouldn't achieve anything because there would be no point in striving for anything. I guess there would be no passion... Yes, okay, I am starting to see how a bit of struggle, and *texture* in life is actually valuable.

NN: Good. The allure of the god realm is a fantasy.

PD: It feels like the end of existence in this realm might be particularly sudden, dramatic and unpleasant. The only place to go from the top is down...

NN: Quite. One version I have heard is that the slightest hint of doubt in a god's mind about the perpetuation of their godly status has an effect. They lose their lustre and start to have a slight smell. This is noticed by the other gods, who move away from them. This increases the doubt and SNAP! Suddenly they are no longer in the god realm.

PD: How could they stay in the god realm?

N'ö: By relaxing. Relaxation and struggle are the means of moving between the realms with regard to the speed of the realms. So if you look at the order of their speed of perception and response—hell, hungry ghost, animal, human, demi-god, god—struggle takes you down to a faster realm, and relaxation—or exhaustion—takes you up into a slower realm.

PD: So if they dismissed the doubt and just relaxed, they would stay in the god realm?

NN: Yes.

Travelling at the Speed of Mind

NN: Shall we move to the demi-gods? This is also called the realm of the jealous gods.

PD: Okay. These are the beings attacking the god realm. They look quite similar to those in the god realm. The main difference is that they are on the ground—not in the clouds and the great tree—and are looking up and attacking the gods. I like that one person has an axe and is attacking the tree where the gods abide.

NN: *[Laughs]* Yes. I like that detail too.

N'ö: Ngak'chang Rinpoche calls these beings: *'avariciously covetous acquisitivists, who are upwardly-mobile, self-centred, manipulative paranoids inhabiting a Machiavellian maze where nothing can be taken at face value and every initiative is a calculated risk that is miscalculated in order to promote status.'*

PD: *[Laughs]* Sounds like middle management.

NN: That is an example that Rinpoche and Khandro Déchen have used. Say you are a manager. You are so focused on getting to the top, so jealous of the status of senior managers, that you will do anything to attain that status for yourself. Although you have a good income, a flash car, a large and beautiful home, an intelligent and capable spouse and lovely children – it is not enough. You must get to the top of the tree where everything will be perfect and then you can relax.

PD: So that is the struggle, the ambition?

NN: Yes. Unfortunately you ignore and neglect what you *actually* have so totally in your striving, that there is no pleasure in being well off, the car, the house, the family. All are neglected in your ambition. You may achieve what you seek, only to eventually discover it is hollow. Or you may suddenly find that you have lost all that you valued through your self-centred acquisitive manipulations – your partner leaves you and takes the children. The house and car are lost in the divorce settlement. The children become estranged.

PD: It's a bit of a cliché, but I can see that sort of pattern at work in my life whenever there is frustration. Something happened the other day that describes this perfectly.

NN: Please say more if you wish.

PD: A friend had created an e-book and sent me a link to buy it. I tried to download it and everything went wrong. I ended up on a porn site and getting locked out of my account. I had to purge my computer, delete all my cookies and do a major system reset. It was most annoying and frustrating.

NN: Oh dear.

PD: I realised later, once I had sorted it all out, that rather than thanking the person who sent me the e-book link, I had sent a message complaining about all the problems I'd encountered as if it was their fault – which it wasn't. I regretted that. Eventually I was able to download it successfully and enjoy the e-book and appreciate the kindness and work of the person who created it.

NN: *[Laughs]* That's quite a story! The regret is wholesome. Regret, make reparations if possible, and then let it go.

PD: Yes. That is what I tried to do.

NN: I think your story illustrates an aspect of the realm very well. There is the feeling of others being responsible for your lack of success – hence *jealous* gods. Someone is hindering your success, either in your realm, or in the realm you aspire to. You are frustrated because your efforts do not bring the desired result.

PD: Someone else gets the promotion…

NN: Quite. And if you ask them how they did it, they just say something vague about being the right person, in the right place, at the right time.

PD: I think that perhaps jealous gods do not actually want to escape their realm because they feel that they have almost made it to the top – they are nearly there.

N'ö: Yes. They feel that just a bit more struggle and they'll cover the last distance and *be* the right person, in the right place, at the right time.

PD: I think it is interesting that there is a great tree between these two realms. It seems significant.

NN: Do say more.

PD: Well the focus on a particular aim is a bit like not being able to see the wood for the trees. There is no sense of enjoying the journey and embracing whatever happens on the journey as part of the whole experience in the jealous god realm. This realm particularly seems to be about losing contact with what is happening now, because I am so focussed on being somewhere else.

NN: That is well expressed.

N'ö: So, the hell and hungry ghost realms are suffering – the demons are your own creation, and it is distorted perception that creates the painful situation. The animal realm beings are dull – numbness and endurance is chosen rather than striving for something better. The gods are oblivious and deluded by the effortlessness of success. And then here, the jealous gods are not suffering like the hell beings or hungry ghosts, and are not dull and numb like the animals, but are blind to what *is* because of their yearning for *what could be*.

PD: So that leaves us with the human realm – the realm that is the most conducive to spiritual practice.

NN: Yes. These are the '*potentially humane-beings*'.

N'ö: In Ngak'chang Rinpoche's words, '*who are creative-destructive, borderline-ironic dilettantes who inhabit the perfect playground of pleasure and pain – in which moments of balance allow an openness to vistas in which change is not necessarily threatening.*'

PD: *Potentially* humane...?

NN: Nothing is guaranteed! How much time do you actually spend in the human realm? The human realm is the realm that has the potential of being a Precious Human rebirth. It has the attributes and freedoms that make practice possible.

Travelling at the Speed of Mind

PD: So *looking* human is not enough – one head, two arms, two legs, five senses, the capacity to discriminate... These could manifest in any of the other realms?

NN: Yes, that's right. But where there is humour and courage – it becomes a Precious Human rebirth. If you are constantly angry and irritated... if you complain continually and never find anything to your satisfaction... if you follow a fashion, a lifestyle, a manner, without choice or examination... if you are so self-satisfied that you never notice the needs of others... if you are consumed by ambition and trample on anything in your way... you may *look* human, but you are not.

PD: In your illustration, the humane beings are in a natural environment with buildings. Two people are ploughing a field with oxen. There is a man in bed who looks like he might be ill. There are prayer flags and a lhakhang and a group are practising with instruments.

N'ö: There is more of an emphasis on practice taking place in the image of this realm.

PD: Is it significant that in the hell and hungry ghost realms the human-looking beings are naked, whilst in the human realm and two god realms they are clothed?

NN: You are more vulnerable and fearful if you are naked. It emphasises the atmosphere of fear and suffering in the hell and hungry ghost realms.

PD: So why is the humane-beings realm the best?

NN: It is the best from the perspective of offering an opportunity to see clearly, to change view, to have a reason to wish to escape, and being able to care about others and wish to help them. There is the potential to see directly, and for appreciation. Also the psycho-physical makeup of a humane being is a perfect vessel for realisation. You have the freedom, opportunity and physical capability to practise silent sitting. You can empty the mind. You are able to appreciate and enter the dimension of the sense fields and the natural elements. There is the possibility of inspiration and focussing on aspiration.

PD: There is more space in this realm, but not too much space?

NN: The experience of striving for satisfaction and experiencing it, or failing to experience it, happens at a speed that enables you to become suspicious of the process. It is not so fast that you cannot see the process—as in the three lower realms—and not so slow that it does not occur to you to question it – as it might in the demi-god and god realms.

PD: You mentioned humour and courage. Could you say more about that please?

NN: Humour is a characteristic of the Precious Human rebirth. A sense of humour opens opportunities to change view and question view. When a situation arises that might create anger, the capacity to let go of subject and object opens the possibility of humour. You were trying to download a Dharma book but ended up on a porn site. That is funny.

PD: Yes it was funny – later on when I'd got over the frustration.

N'ö: Here's another example: I get all dressed up to go to a fancy restaurant, pay a lot of money for the meal, and then it is mediocre to say the least. That is funny.

NN: It may not feel particularly funny at the time – until you allow a spacious gap to arise and look at the situation. So now an example of courage: when everyone around me is joining in the character assassination of someone I know, it is courageous to offer an alternative positive viewpoint.

N'ö: Or… when I have an important meeting that might mean a promotion, it is courageous to let them know that I will not be attending because I have to help my neighbour who has had an accident and needs me to take them to hospital.

NN: It is courageous to see humour in difficult life circumstances. It is humorous to take the courageous route when it may jeopardise everything you thought would make you happy. When everything is good for me: I am well-off, can afford whatever I need, and have people with me who love me, it is humane to notice that others are not so fortunate, and wish to help them.

PD: So you have to try to stay in the humane-beings realm?

N'ö: Absolutely. If courage becomes distorted into aggression, then the realm is lost. If humour is distorted into laughing *at* rather than laughing *with* – then the realm is lost. The Precious Human rebirth is the realm of practice where you can stay on the path to awakening or fall into the path of delusion.

NN: Similarly, a gap or opening of view in any of the other realms could instantly transport you to the human realm with its benefits, attributes and potential.

PD: I have noticed that in each realm there is a scene where the beings seem to be receiving teachings, and also that there is a Buddha-like figure in each realm.

NN: Yes. This is an expression of the reality that escape from any realm is always possible. There is no such thing as a lost cause in Buddhism. No being is so deluded, so depraved, has committed so much evil that there is no hope of reversal. Everything can be transformed.

PD: So if we cultivate right view and action, we can escape?

NN: Yes. Karma does not have to be worked out deed by deed, thought by thought, emotion by emotion. Spontaneous awakening is available in every moment. Realised mind is beginningless, is always present and always available, but occluded by ignorance, patterning and deluded response. A moment of space opens up a possibility for any being in any realm to hear or realise a new perspective.

PD: The teachers in each realm look like the beings of that realm…

N'ö: Yes. This makes them approachable for those beings in those realms. The teachers need to be in a form that the beings of the realm can understand.

PD: And the Buddhas…?

N'ö: These are the Six Sages, or Six Munis. You may have noticed that they are different colours?

PD: Yes. In the hell realm the Buddha—sage—is black, in the hungry ghost realm blue, in the animal realm red, in the god realm white, in the jealous god realm green, and in the human realm yellow.

NN: That is how they appear in this thangka, though I think it is more usual to reverse the colours of the animal and hungry ghost realm sages. The hungry ghost realm sage would be red and the animal realm sage blue. The black sage of the hell realm is Yama Dharmaraja, King of Dharma.

PD: That is the same being who holds the Wheel?

NN: Yes.

PD: But that is surely the one who is teaching, rather than the sage?

N'ö: They are the same. One is the teacher appearing in a form the student can understand. The other is the teacher as a sage. A hell being would not be able to comprehend a Buddha-like figure, but Yama Dharmaraja is within the scope of their perception.

PD: He seems to be holding a flame.

NN: He is usually depicted holding a flame and a conch shell of water – each to ease the extremes of the hell realms: to warm and melt icy menace and to cool and quench burning hatred. These symbolise the possibility of transforming hellish experience.

PD: Could you run through the others, please?

NN: The sage in the hungry ghost realm is called Jvalamukha. Usually red, this sage holds a casket of treasures to overcome the miserliness, lack of appreciation and sense of impoverishment of the hungry ghost realm. The animal realm Buddha is usually blue and holding a book to overcome the ignorance of the animal realm. He is called Sthirasimha – the Steadfast Lion.

PD: The red sage seems to be holding a treasure vase?

N'ö: Yes, it looks like that in this thangka.

NN: Perhaps a mistake was made in the painting and the sages for these realms have been reversed. A treasure vase is a reasonable version of a casket of treasures, but in the wrong realm.

PD: The white god realm sage is holding a musical instrument. What does that signify?

N'ö: This is Indrasakra – Indra, the Lord of the Gods. A note played on an instrument is pure throughout its duration, but then the oscillation that creates the sound dies and the note just ends. Indrasakra plays the lute to remind the gods of impermanence.

NN: The sage of the jealous god realm is Vemacitra – Splendid Robe. He is holding a mandala offering in this thangka but is usually shown holding armour and weaponry. Finally the sage of the human realm is a more familiar figure: Sakyamuni – the Lion of the Shakya clan, who is holding an alms bowl.

PD: So this is like the manifestation of Guru Rinpoche as a mendicant?

N'ö: Yes.

PD: Could I just quickly ask about the other order of viewing the realms – in terms of speed?

NN: Yes, please do.

PD: I can see that the hell realm is really fast with regard to perception and response, and that the hungry ghost realm is pretty fast. The animal realm does not seem so fast though – in fact it feels slower than the humane-beings and demi-gods.

NN: It is the speed of the recurrence of the mind-pattern of the realm, and the speed of the recurrence of dissatisfaction that is in question.

N'ö: The speed of the turning of the wheel in terms of a cycle of dissatisfaction, increases as you move through the realms from the gods to the hells.

NN: So the hell realms are the fastest, then the hungry ghost realm, animal realm, human realm, jealous god realm, and then finally the slowest is the god realm which could feel so satisfying for so long that they may believe they are realised. To return to the animal realm in terms of speed, relative to the higher realms, the pain is not so graphic and intense as in the hell realm and hungry ghost realm – but it is perpetual. Their view and opinion is so fixed that the herd mentality of remaining with that view is continuous – that is the speed of it.

N'ö: Seeking security in belonging to whatever is the mode of your herd, requires constant application. You have to be sure of the current fashion and conform. You have to continually seek reassurances that your view is satisfactory and swell the numbers who support it in order to suppress any other view. You must amass territory for your view and undermine the territory of any other view. There is no possibility of questioning what is satisfaction; what is dissatisfaction.

NN: So in this way the experience of dissatisfaction cycles faster in the animal realm than in the three higher realms.

PD: Okay. I get that now thanks. Then, with the humane-beings realm I can see the balance of being able to sort-of look sideways and question view and opinion. There is a willingness to entertain challenge and to change. There is the possibility—as you said—of humour and courage. But then we move to the demi-god realm, which seems quite speedy again. In what way is it slower than the previous realms?

NN: The beings themselves may be energetic, but it is the speed of the *cycle of samsara* that is slower. Jealous gods achieve satisfaction—they make it to middle management—but it is not quite enough for them.

N'ö: They are ambitious and they believe they can make samsara work. Humane beings recognise that they cannot really make samsara work and this is why there is humour and courage, but jealous gods are poised on the brink.

NN: Jealous gods lose the capacity for seeing humour in their situation because they think that they *can* make samsara work if they can just overcome the obstacles.

PD: Right. I see. The god realm is easy to see as very slow and protracted. I think it is good to look at that view of the realms as well. It helps me understand why the realm of the Precious Human rebirth is so important.

NN: Good.

PD: Do you have an example of how you might move through the realms in terms of ordinary experience?

NN: Hmmm… let me see. How about this:

> *What a beautiful morning* – humane realm.
> *Oh, this is a horrible mess left in the bathroom* – hot hell.
> *Oh, you've received a gift in the post from our friend have you – just for you?* – jealous god.
> *Huh. That's not fair. I wanted one of those. Why didn't they send me one? Well I don't care – it's a rather cheap and nasty version anyway* – hungry ghost.
> *Idiot! What am I doing? I'm so happy to see their enjoyment of their gift* – humane realm.
> *Phew! Back to being human in time for breakfast!*

PD: *[Laughs]* I like that.

NN: Good. And now, it is time for bed. It has been quite an intense day. I do not think that there is so much to say about the next two sections of the Wheel, so tomorrow's two sessions will not be so long.

PD: Thank you very much, Ngakma-la, Ngakpa-la. Goodnight.

NN & N'ö: Goodnight.

NN: Do make a drink before you go to bed if you wish.

N'ö: Sleep well, and we'll see you in the morning.

6 – Going Up or Going Down

A new day has dawned. Ngakma Nor'dzin, Ngakpa 'ö-Dzin, and Pema Dorje have finished their morning meditation practice. They have enjoyed a good breakfast and been out for a walk. Now they are ready to return to their examination of the Wheel of Life.

NN: There is not so much to say about the next part of the thangka, so it does not matter that we are starting this session quite late into the morning.

PD: It was good to stretch our legs and get out into the sunshine.

NN: It was. So this ring is not included on every thangka of the Wheel of Life, but when included, it sits between the central circular hub and the ring of the six realms.

PD: Why would it not always be included?

NN: The other details of the Wheel naturally include the meaning of this ring.

PD: So—to examine it—the ring is divided vertically into two halves. The left side is light and has white clouds, and the right side is black. On the left side there are people on the clouds who look like practitioners. One of them is holding a rosary and a prayer wheel. On the cloud at the top of this section is another Buddha-like figure. The indication is an upward direction moving towards the Buddha figure.

NN: This describes the results of spiritual practice: progressing towards awakening.

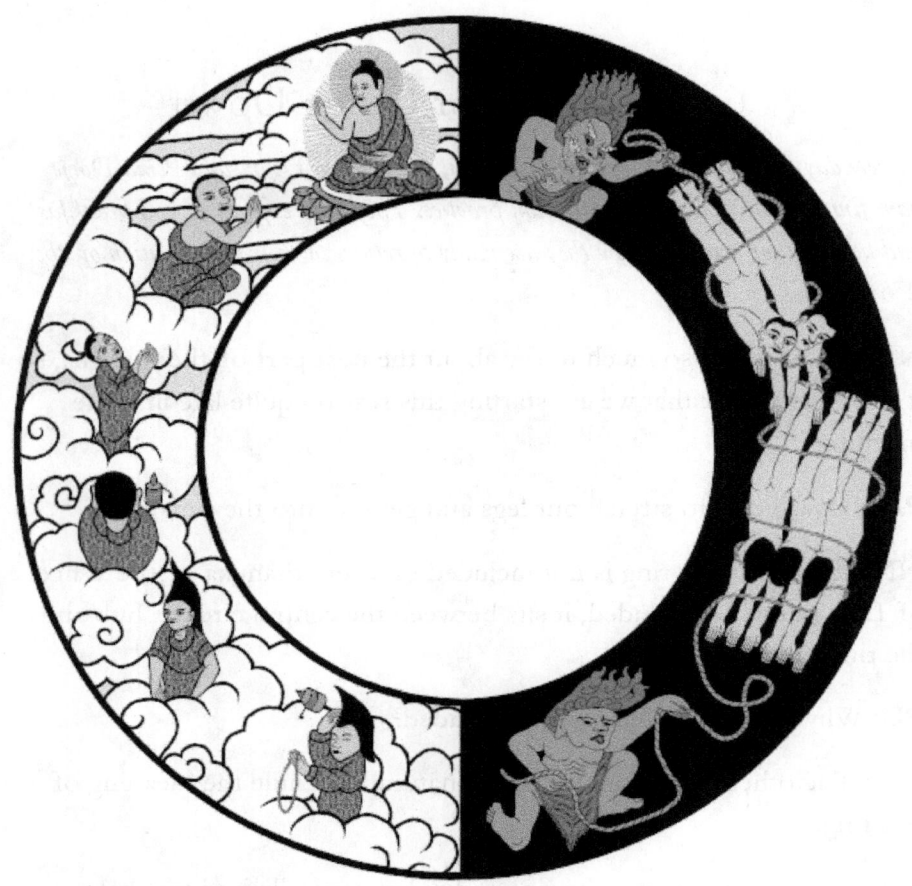

PD: The other black half of the ring has a blue demon at the top and a red demon at the bottom who are dragging naked, bound people downwards.

NN: This describes the results of negative actions and mindstates – falling into the lower realms, dragged by your own demonic patterning.

PD: It communicates the message clearly. Does the red demon represent the hot hells and the blue demon the cold hells?

N'ö: That is a question that we have never asked, but that sounds perfectly reasonable.

NN: I have noticed that in some renditions—such as the Wheel of Life at Bartsham lhakhang in East Bhutan—that there are ten clouds on the left side, each with a practitioner upon it. This indicates the ten stages of progression of a Bodhisattva until full realisation. These ten stages are connected to the ten perfections.

PD: The word 'sin' is not really used in Buddhism, is it, but these feel like descriptions of the results of either virtue or sin.

NN: That is certainly one way of understanding this ring. Buddhism talks about 'error' or 'mistake' rather than 'sin', and teaches basic goodness – that human beings are fundamentally wholesome, but confused view and ignorance causes mistakes to be made.

PD: Is that because the badness a person might do is seen as harming oneself as much as harming another?

N'ö: Yes. Remember the hell realms… the demons torturing the hell realm beings are their own distortion and patterning.

NN: 'Delusion', 'confusion', or 'neurosis' might also be used instead of the word 'sin'.

PD: So thinking about the other side—the side of virtue and morality—I guess the word 'merit' would be used here?

N'ö: 'Merit' is sometimes not understood very clearly by Buddhists. The idea of 'accumulating merit' can be seen as putting pennies in a piggy bank.

PD: *[Laughs]* How would you describe merit?

NN: Well it is not so much merit itself that is not understood, but more the concept of 'accumulating merit'.

PD: So am I right in thinking that merit is all the moments of awareness, kindness, generosity, patience, forbearance – all the actions and attitudes that have a lack of selfishness at their core.

NN: Yes – all the qualities described by the ten perfections. If wisdom prevails there is no error, and response will naturally be compassionate. If compassion prevails there will be no error, and wisdom will naturally be present.

PD: So… about accumulating merit… in Sutrayana, meritorious action is emphasised to undermine the focus on oneself, in order to discover emptiness of self.

N'ö: Exactly. So you could say that the path of Sutrayana works on changing the view and actions of the practitioner to develop a view of emptiness of self. So for example, anger may be purified by contemplating that every being will have been your mother at some point in the endless cycle of rebirths, and cared for you. Alternatively, you may analyse the relationship between oneself, and a friend, an enemy, and a stranger, in order to recognise the centrality of oneself in those definitions. You may focus on generating loving kindness toward the object of your anger as an antidote.

PD: And it is this method of practice that is regarded as meritorious and is accumulated?

NN: Precisely. So if you cannot control an emotion, you remove yourself from situations that incite that emotion, and meditate on the antidote. Sutrayana emphasises the accumulation of merit because the practice is to replace erroneous responses with meritorious responses. The erroneous views and responses are examined and weeded out through analysis and through contemplating their antidotes.

PD: But Vajrayana starts with the experience of emptiness and works towards understanding emptiness and form as a nonduality?

N'ö: Exactly. This is achieved by allowing form to be what it is. The relationship with form is changed through seeing form directly and accurately, not through analysis or applying antidotes.

PD: So that is why Vajrayana uses symbolic form, because that cannot be manipulated?

NN: That's right. In Vajrayana form is not considered to be a problem – it does not need to be controlled in order to avoid the arising of erroneous responses. The erroneous responses themselves are used as the focus of practice, so that the energy of a response can be transformed into nondual experience and liberated. You do not have to remove yourself from that which stimulates a response, in fact you welcome it.

PD: But a Vajrayana practitioner would still wish to engage in activities that are considered meritorious, such as kindness, generosity, and so on – the ten perfections?

NN: Of course.

PD: So what is the difference?

NN: Well there is no difference in terms of the act of kindness or generosity itself.

PD: So is the difference the view?

NN: Yes. Here is a rather clumsy analogy. If you have a garden full of weeds, the Sutrayana approach is to take out the weeds one at a time and replace them with the desired plants. The Vajrayana approach would be to regard 'weed' as an unnecessary classification and to simply enjoy the plants for what they are. You can encourage some more than others, and move them around, but all the plants are regarded as potentially beautiful and desirable in the garden.

PD: Okay. So, to get back to this part of the Wheel of Life that we are examining… a moment of purity, awakening, realisation, open-hearted wholesomeness—whatever you want to call it—will put you on that cloudy highway?

N'ö: Yes. It will be a moment of dropping the structure that supports the illusion of self-existence.

PD: But you can't store that moment.

NN: Exactly. That is the point. However having had that moment, that experience, makes it part of the potential of your mindstream. It becomes easier to have such a moment again.

PD: It is like starting a habit – but a good habit.

NN: Yes. It is skilful and leads in the direction of awakening.

PD: It is all the same though really, isn't it? All paths lead to the Buddha cloud at the top?

NN: *[Laughs]* It is all the same – to the person who can see that it is all the same. If your life is hell, and your whole experience is fear/defend/attack, then the pattern is so fast it is difficult to see and almost impossible to cut. A moment of noticing the fear in your attacker, however, and questioning that in your mind, might create a tiny pause of openness that is free of the fear/defend/attack pattern.

PD: And that might be enough to open the possibility of a different view, a different realm?

NN: Exactly.

PD: Could we go back to the idea of accumulating merit? I can see how it cannot be an accumulation in the ordinary sense, like savings in a bank, but progress *is* made. Is it about momentum?

NN: Yes – momentum in the sense of increasing the frequency of moments of awakening activity and view.

PD: Practices in liturgical traditions usually begin with a verse which is the generation of Bodhicitta and end with the dedication of merit.

N'ö: This is to do with intention. It is a bit like saying: '*I'm going to do this practice because I want to be a person who benefits others.*' And then at the end: '*I have completed this practice in order to be a person who benefits others.*'

NN: The intention is manifested, followed through, and celebrated. That is a complete karma.

PD: Ah yes. I can see that. To be complete and create a pattern in the mindstream, there must be the intention to act, the action, and the satisfaction of having completed the action.

N'ö: So generation of Bodhicitta at the beginning of the practice, and dedication at the end, are a formalised method of creating a complete karmic pattern of practice.

NN: It is so important to be conscientious about practice intentions. If you decide to practise for an hour, try to follow that through. If that is really hard for you, it would be better to have an intention to practise for twenty minutes and achieve that every day, than set an intention that is beyond your capacity. Every action starts or adds to patterning. Continually giving up on personal intentions is not a useful pattern to keep supporting. A practitioner needs to be a person of honour, a person who keeps their word, and is reliable – in all areas of life. Being honourable about practice intention is part of that. You need to be able to trust yourself.

PD: So this is what is meant by accumulating merit to advance up those holy clouds of progression towards awakening!

NN: Hallelujah!

[Laughter]

PD: The method—in terms of karma and patterning—is exactly the same on the other side, isn't it?

NN: It is. If the intention is based in delusion, there is still intention that is manifested, followed through, and celebrated, creating a complete karma. In this instance, however, the intention is unskilful and will create or deepen a pattern of delusion, leading to further entrenchment in samsara.

N'ö: It could be described as generation of deluded intention, deluded action, and dedication of the completion of one's deluded intention.

PD: So that describes the path on the black side of this ring. I guess the trick is to try to do the white side karmic patterning more than the black side karmic patterning?

NN: Well yes… but that is still a rather materialistic approach. That is still in the sphere of the balance scales, or piggy bank. It is the *present moment* that is the key and the important factor.

N'ö: This ring seems to provide a sort of overview – a general approach to how to conduct yourself. An overview is more useful than no view at all—in terms of progress towards awakening—but spontaneity is the most profound approach. Remember that this image, the Wheel of Life, is a Sutrayana presentation of cyclic existence. It describes the gradual path. Progress is slow and systematic in the Sutrayana approach. The path of Sutrayana is the renunciation of the causes of cyclic existence, and the fruit is the realisation of the emptiness of the self.

NN: Remember this image is on the *outside* of the lhakhang. The Wheel of Life teaching has to be accessible from an experientially common base that is available to everyone – the base of Sutrayana.

PD: Whereas in Vajrayana you start with emptiness?

NN: Yes, which is not so accessible as an experiential base of practice. There needs to be a teacher, and some understanding of emptiness.

PD: Thinking back to when we talked about the twelve links of interdependent origination—and the skandhas—arising in a 500th of a second… and that you are born into one of the realms for that mind moment…

NN: Yes.

PD: Is this basically saying the same thing? Am I in the humane-being realm, or am I in a hell realm? Am I on a cloud elevator at this moment or am I bound and being dragged down?

NN: *[Laughs]* Certainly. Mind moments and actions can be described as skilful or unskilful. Skilful moments lead to awakening; unskilful moments compound being asleep. But this ring is describing a trend rather than a moment. It is not describing jumping between these two states continually.

PD: So you need to keep intention rooted in openness and kindness and that keeps you on the holy highway.

N'ö: Yes. If you are able to have awareness and appropriate intention in the present moment, then everything will take care of itself. There is no need for gradual weeding, because there will be moments of instantaneous transformation. It is the frequency that increases.

PD: So there is actually only one cloud?

NN: *[Laughs]* Yes: nonduality.

PD: I think I've heard this ring in the Wheel of Life explained as illustrating the bardo state – the state between rebirths.

NN: Yes, I have heard that as well. Bardo means 'intermediary state'. It is the period between rebirths, between each cycle of the Wheel, when there is a potential gap – a bardo. If that is the case, then this ring would be describing the period of transition – the direction of travel that has been created through the bardo between cycles.

PD: Could you say that the whole of the Wheel is describing a bardo – a point in time when the Wheel is still and can be examined.

NN: That could be one way of looking at it. This ring is a bit like a warning, and a reminder of impermanence. What direction of travel is being established right now, in this life at this moment?

N'ö: The images of the realms address the state of being in that realm, and illustrate the benefits of the human realm. The links describe the process of arriving in a realm – at whatever speed you are working. This ring describes the direction of merit and error. These do not describe the actual patterns of the realms that need to be overcome.

NN: That is true. The causes of patterning are described by the links, the results of patterning are the realms, and the central hub illustrates the three root misconceptions – the driving force of the Wheel.

PD: So this ring reinforces the message that you need to stay in the Precious Human realm and work on overcoming fundamental ignorance?

NN: Yes. Indeed. Well, I don't think there's any more to say about that section of the Wheel of Life. We seem to be ready to move to discussing the central hub.

N'ö: Shall we have a tea break, and reconvene in half an hour?

NN & PD: Yes.

NN: That is an excellent idea.

The Central Hub

7 – The Central Hub

There is not much time remaining before the weekend is over and Pema Dorje must return home. There is only one more section of the Wheel of Life to discuss, however, and the three retreatants settle down for their final session together.

N'ö: So the final part of the Wheel to discuss is the central hub.

PD: This has a bird, a pig, and a snake who all seem to be chasing each other. They are biting each others' tails.

PD: Well a snake is a slithery sort of creature and often represents something bad in folklore. It is the one of the three that could be venomous and have a dangerous bite. So I think this is hatred.

NN: Correct again. The term we usually use is 'aversion'. Hatred is too emotive and does not encompass the scope and range of aversion. You may not hate that it's raining, but if it is irritating – there is aversion.

PD: So this leaves the cockerel, who is a rather noisy and showy bird, who struts around the courtyard looking pleased with himself. This is desire or pride.

NN: So you did know which was which. The preferred term here is 'attraction', again because it covers the entire range of a slight preference to slathering lust.

PD: In the interdependent links, ignorance was a blind person. Here it is a pig…?

N'ö: Ignorance in the links is *fundamental ignorance* – the mistake of believing in an inherently self-existing 'I'.

NN: Here the ignorance is *wilful ignorance* – a misconceived response.

N'ö: The ignorance of the pig is *ignore*-ance. It is a choice of reaction to perception.

PD: So these three are right in the centre of the Wheel, at the hub, so they must be very important. I think they must be like the powerhouse that makes the Wheel turn?

N'ö: That's right. These three are the reactions that create entrapment in the realms. I am attracted to something that I think I will like, that I think will make me happy.

NN: I am averse to something I don't like, or seems to threaten me in some way.

N'ö: Indifference regards the situation as of no interest or relevance to the sense of self, when it does not appear to promise happiness or forebode unhappiness. It is therefore ignored.

NN: It is the fixation with individuated identity that creates a problem. **I** want it, don't want it, or don't care.

N'ö: We are always examining how does this situation impact on *me*? Is it going to make *me* happy or unhappy, or is it irrelevant to *me*?

PD: So—to check I've got this right—we always start from indifference and then react either with attraction or aversion. If it doesn't seem to be about *me*, I am indifferent. As soon as the possibility arises of it being about *me* – there is attraction or aversion.

N'ö: Yes. The key factor is the focus on *me*. Everything is analysed and classified according to its relevance to *me*. It is a fundamental misunderstanding of reality – *everything* is relevant because *everything* is totally interconnected.

PD: And we are all doing this all the time? I continually analyse whether something is good for me, bad for me, or makes no difference to me?

NN: Yes.

PD: I think one of the problems for me with this teaching, is that I don't feel that I am judging, classifying and reacting like this all the time…

N'ö: Yes, you are so habituated to it, it is such a habit, that it feels normal and natural – you don't see that you are doing it. It is the same for everyone. That is why learning to dwell in emptiness is so important. It provides the space to see the pattern or process. You start to see that you make a judgement and a decision, and then respond based on that decision in every mind moment.

NN: Yes. And having made the decision about good, bad, or not interested, you then respond with attraction, aversion, or indifference. You are attracted to anything that you think will make you happy, and you want more and more of it. You might also want to stop others having it. You are averse to anything that you think will make you unhappy, and if that something keeps happening you have to destroy it. If something doesn't seem to impact upon your happiness or unhappiness, then you just ignore it until you need to give it your attention.

PD: Another problem I have with this, is that it *does* actually feel like I am at the centre of everything.

NN: It does. You are right. This is because you feel that there is a self-existing 'I' that owns your experience. The teachings, and particularly the practices that develop an experience of emptiness, enable you to release that feeling of ownership. Perception happens. The senses sense. Emotions arise, abide and dissolve.

N'ö: There does not need to be a *me* owning and controlling that process.

PD: I see. So to get back to the image of these three animals, why are they biting each other's tails?

N'ö: This is to indicate a connection, a circle, rather than that they are attacking one another.

NN: They are usually depicted in this way, in my experience, but I have seen one or two versions of the Wheel of Life, where the snake and the cockerel seem to be coming out of the mouth of the pig.

PD: Why would that be?

NN: Ignorance or indifference is the primary state from which attraction or aversion might arise.

PD: Could you say a bit more?

NN: It is simply emphasising the *me-centric* nature of the process. Most of the time we are like the pig, ignoring things and indifferent to them. Once something impacts upon us we respond – we either like it or don't like it, we are attracted to it or averse. The pig only cares about itself.

N'ö: As you said, the pig experiences itself as being the centre of everything and as the most important being in the world. The world rotates around it. So it ignores you and everyone else, unless something happens that makes it feel happy or unhappy, attracted or averse, and then it pays attention.

NN: If whatever happens seems to be able to make the pig happy then it spews out the cockerel—or arises in the form of the cockerel—and struts around crowing about the situation. But if the pig thinks the situation will make it unhappy or feels threatened in some way, then it spews out the snake—or arises in the form of the snake—and rears up hissing, spits venom, and bites. Both the cockerel and the snake are still the pig, just with a costume on to let you know how it thinks about you.

PD: You know, that it is so simple and obvious but I have never thought of it. If I'm in a room full of people I will have no sense of connection or reaction to them if there is no interaction. It is as if they do not exist until something brings them into focus. When I go for a walk I probably fail to notice 90% of the environment. We do walk around in a state of dull indifference to almost everything around us. I feel quite shocked, recognising this.

NN: I quite like that version of the image – the cockerel and snake coming out of the pig's mouth. I think it is instructive.

PD: Now this has set me on a train of thought. May I explore this with you?

N'ö: Yes, of course.

PD: Does this alternative way of depicting the three animals have something to do with Sutrayana and Vajrayana? In Sutrayana, the causes of attraction and aversion are avoided through practising renunciation, whereas in Vajrayana they are embraced?

NN: Go on.

PD: So is the path of Sutrayana to remain with indifference as a less harmful state, avoiding attraction and aversion?

NN: A less harmful state…? Indifference can be just as harmful as attraction and aversion.

N'ö: Indifference can include callousness, lack of concern for others, and insensitivity.

NN: It could be not caring, and wishing not to get involved when help could be offered – such as walking by when a child or elderly person falls over in the street.

PD: But doesn't Sutrayana work with calming things down – like indifference, whereas Vajrayana works with energy – like attraction and aversion? I mean, if there is no reaction, then this is possibly better than greedy self-centred attraction, or than malicious self-centred aversion.

NN: This sounds like an attempt to make the image fit an idea. Indifference is also renounced in Sutrayana. Indifference is also engaged in Vajrayana.

N'ö: The three root misconceptions are relevant in Sutrayana and Vajrayana. It is the method that changes. Sutrayana works through the principle of renunciation. Vajrayana works through the principle of transformation.

PD: But I was thinking that the imagery is so energetic and dynamic in Vajrayana…?

NN: That is true, but your train of thought is extrapolating in the wrong direction. There are peaceful, joyous and wrathful practices in Vajrayana which can be equated to working with indifference, attraction, and aversion. Sutrayana also works with all three, but through renunciation rather than transformation.

N'ö: The pig represents *wilful* ignorance—an active decision to ignore—and that would not be regarded as a preferable state in any path of Buddhist practice.

PD: Okay. I can see how I am trying to create a pattern again, but if I am stuck with patterning and reactivity—until I have the capacity to let that go or transform it—might it be better to be a cockerel as much as possible and not let the snake out?

NN: *[Laughs]* Do say more.

PD: Well… if I try to be a friend to everyone and look for how everything could make me happy, maybe that would not be so bad. If I find I can't do that, then it would be better to stay a pig and ignore them, than to let the snake out and bite them – at least until I could get back to being a cockerel.

NN: Let's take that apart a little… if you are trying to be a friend to everyone, there is selflessness in that. Being a friend to everyone would involve renouncing—or letting go—of minor irritations and upsets that got in the way of that. This would be skilful activity.

N'ö: If you try to avoid being unpleasant to people and avoid fostering unpleasant attitudes to others – that is also letting go, and skilful activity.

NN: If you have sufficient awareness that your reaction might be more in the direction of harming than helping, so you decide to ignore or exit the situation – that is also renunciation and skilful activity.

N'ö: If being a cockerel includes focusing on how you can make others happy, this has gone beyond self-centred attraction and moved towards loving kindness. Your cockerel is on the cloudy highway.

PD: In what way would focusing on being a cockerel be just as self-centred and harmful?

NN: Wanting or taking more than your fair share… going for your own needs and desires and being oblivious to others' needs and desires… taking pleasure out of something that is clearly harming someone else… and so on.

PD: Ah yes. I see.

N'ö: You are actually talking about noble and kind intention. It could be that simple and direct. Be nice to everyone. It might not always work, but if you try to be nice and other people are not nice back, maybe you could just not let that bother you.

PD: Somehow it feels that if I opened up more, then appreciation and greater happiness would naturally be there.

NN: Appreciation is the result of transformed attraction – limitless, unbounded appreciation for everyone and everything, everywhere.

PD: So… to check my understanding, instead of filtering all experience through its relevance to supporting, threatening, or having nothing to do with *me*—my sense of an inherent self—I could experience and appreciate everything just as it is?

N'ö: Yes. If it is painful, it is painful. If it is joyful, it is joyful. It is *as it is*, free of the structure that requires attraction, aversion or indifference. Free of the structure of feeling that because something is being experienced by *me*, *I* must be the most important thing in the universe.

NN: This is why opening the sense fields is such an important practice. Dullness of the sense fields is an aspect of indifference – we close down and cut off.

N'ö: Remembering to actively keep the sense fields open can help overcome disconnection and indifference.

PD: So that is just trying to be aware and open – noticing and appreciating whatever is experienced through the senses?

NN: Yes.

PD: Everything really is *so* interesting if I pay attention.

NN: We need the wisdom of the elderly and the wonderment of the very young. Children do not suffer from indifference quite like adults. They have a sense of wonder and curiosity, and a willingness to not know and be bewildered without being overwhelmed. Adults could retain this childlike quality of appreciation and interest in anything and everything.

N'ö: Sadly it seems to be expected that adults grow out of the wonder and appreciation of all phenomena. Adults tend to limit the scope of their appreciation, and slip into either not caring or developing strong opinions about what is not liked. We could simply *play* or *dance* with experience rather than solidifying it. We could remain fluid, rather than consolidating preferences and opinions.

PD: So, I think we have come to the end of what needs to be asked about attraction, aversion and indifference.

N'ö: And we are running out of time now.

PD: So, to quickly recap… the ignorance in the links is the base ignorance that sets the whole cycle in motion?

NN: That's right. That initial wrong view that there is something permanent and self-existing that owns mental formations, consciousness, the skandhas, and the senses, sets the whole thing in motion. It is this ground delusion that leads to craving and grasping at sensation once contact with phenomena has been made.

PD: And this causes rebirth in one of the realms.

N'ö: Yes. Attraction, aversion and indifference act as the continual confirmation of the belief in a self-existing 'I', powering the Wheel, and keeping cyclic existence revolving.

PD: It seems to me that there opportunities within the cycle described in the Wheel, to cut the pattern.

NN: There are. Taking these opportunities leads to the white path and awakening. Squandering these opportunities in favour of deluded indulgences leads to the black path.

N'ö: And Yama—to go right back to the beginning of our discussions—holds the Wheel to show us these opportunities.

PD: Death—or emptiness—is the key – seeing that change is possible and pattern can be liberated.

NN: Yes. Yama, the Lord of Death, holds the Wheel to insist we look, understand, and practise to discover emptiness.

PD: Wow… It has been quite a journey this weekend – looking at the Wheel of Life in such depth. Thank you.

NN & N'ö: You are welcome.

NN: I hope it has been helpful – and enjoyable.

PD: Indeed it has.

NN: So we'll have some lunch and then there will be a little time before you need to leave to catch your train.

N'ö: Let's sing Dorje Tsig Dün together and sit for a while – each are profound opportunities to discover a moment of nonduality.

Ngakma Nor'dzin, Ngakpa 'ö-Dzin, and Pema Dorje sing Dorje Tsig Dün—the seven thunderbolt phrases of Guru Rinpoche—to the Vajra Melody called the 'Flight of the Vulture'. Their eyes are wide open and their voices clear and ringing. Then they sit in silence.

7 – *The Central Hub*

The midday sun floods the shrine room with rays of sunlight. The bright rays of light pick up the details of the thangka painted in gold. The Wheel of Life shines – as if it is happy for the attention it has received over the weekend, and as if in appreciation that its message has been embraced and understood.

Glossary

Glossary

Note: 'Tib.' indicates the term in Tibetan / Dharma script. 'Woj.' indicates the transliteration of the term using the Wojkowitz format where the root letter is capitalised when the syllable has a prefix or suffix. 'Skt.' indicates the term in Sanskrit.

accumulating merit

A Sutrayana practice of continual repetition of skilful actions to correct the patterning of unskilful actions.

animal realm being

Tib. དུད་འགྲོ་ Woj. dud 'gro; Skt. tiryak.

antidote

The Sutrayana antidotes to the three root misconceptions are: wisdom to overcome ignorance and indifference (Tib. ཤེས་རབ་ Woj. shes rab; Skt. amoha or prajna); generosity to overcome desire and attachment (Tib. སྦྱིན་པ་ Woj. sByin pa; Skt. alobha or dana); and loving kindness to overcome hatred and aversion (Tib. བྱམས་པ་ Woj. byams pa; Skt. advesa or metta). *See:* root misconceptions.

appropriation

The term used in the Rice Seedling Sutra for 'grasping'.

Aro gTér Lineage

The Aro gTér (Tib ཨ་རོ་གཏེར་ Woj. A ro gTer) is a Nyingma Lineage of Himalayana Buddhism. The teachings of the Aro gTér descend from a lineage of enlightened women, beginning with Yeshé Tsogyel (Tib. ཡེ་ཤེས་མཚོ་རྒྱལ་ Woj. ye shes mTsho rGyal). She was the female Tantric Buddha, who, together with Guru Rinpoche, founded the Nyingma tradition of Buddhism.

The Aro gTér is a small family lineage within that tradition founded by the female visionary Lama, Aro Lingma, in 1909.

Aro Lingma

Tib. ཨ་རོ་གླིང་མ་ Woj. A ro gling ma (1886–1923). Founder of the Aro gTer Lineage. Aro Lingma was a pure-vision gTértön (Tib. གཏེར་སྟོན་ Woj. gTer sTon) – a discoverer of spiritual treasures. She received several cycles of practice directly from Yeshé Tsogyel, the female Buddha and consort of Guru Rinpoche.

astrological

Astrology (Tib. དཀར་རྩིས་ Woj. dKar rTsis) is one of the 'Ten Sciences' (Tib. རིག་པའི་གནས་བཅུ་ Woj. rig pa'i gNas bCu; Skt. dasavidya). These are: arts, grammar, medicine, logic, Buddhism, astrology, poetics, prosody, synonymics, and drama. The astrological cycle is a span of sixty years: a rotation of twelve animals, five elements, and alternating male and female gender.

attraction

Tib. འདོད་ཆགས་ Woj. 'dod chags; Skt. raga. *See:* root misconceptions.

aversion

Tib. ཞེ་སྡང་ Woj. zhe sDang; Skt. dvesa. *See:* root misconceptions.

awakening

The development of realisation; gaining enlightenment. The dualistic, deluded state of beings trapped in cyclic existence is said to be as if asleep, and unaware of the true nature of all beings.

awareness being

Tib ཡི་དམ་ Woj. yi dam; Skt. deva. Visionary beings used as the method of transformation in Vajrayana practice. There are three types: peaceful (Tib. ཞི་ zhi; Skt. zama), joyous (Tib. དགའ་ Woj. dGa; Skt. rata), and wrathful (Tib. ཁྲོ་བོ་ Woj. khro bo; Skt. krodha).

bardo

Tib. བར་དོ་ Woj. bar do; Skt. antarabhava. An intermediary state. 'Bar' means movement or flow, like a stream; and 'do' means an island or rock in the stream. There is an area amidst movement; a gap, gestalt, time frame, or pool of temporal space.

becoming

Tib. སྲིད་པ་ Woj. srid pa; Skt. bhava. One of the twelve interdependent links of origination.

Beer, Robert

A Western thangka painter who studied under Jampa of Dharamsala and Khamtrül Rinpoche of Tashijong. He is the author of several books including 'The Handbook of Tibetan Buddhist Symbols', and 'The Encyclopedia of Tibetan Symbols and Motifs'. I had a brief chat and email conversation with him with regard to the Wheel of Life.

bhumis, ten

Tib. ས་བཅུ་ Woj. sa bCu; Skt. dasa bhumi.
1. Very Joyous: Tib. རབ་ཏུ་དགའ་བ་ Woj. rab tu dGa'ba; Skt. pramudita;
2. Stainless: Tib. དྲི་མ་མེད་པ་ Woj. dri ma med pa; Skt. vimala;
3. Luminous; Tib. འོད་བྱེད་པ་ Woj. 'od byed pa; Skt. prabhakari;
4. Blazing Light; Tib. འོད་འཕྲོ་བ་ Woj. 'od 'phro ba; Skt. arcismati;
5. Difficult to Master; Tib. སྦྱང་དཀའ་བ་ Woj. sByang dKa' ba; Skt. sudurjaya; 6. Realised; Tib. མངོན་དུ་བྱེད་པ་ Woj. mNgon du byed pa; Skt. abhimukhi; 7. Gone Afar; Tib. རིང་དུ་སོང་བ་ Woj. ring du song ba; Skt. duramgama; 8. Immovable: Tib. མི་གཡོ་བ་ Woj. mi g.yo ba; Skt. acala; 9. Good Intelligence: Tib. ལེགས་པའི་བློ་གྲོས་ Woj. legs pa'i bLo gros; Skt. sadhumati; 10. Cloud of Doctrine; Tib. ཆོས་ཀྱི་སྤྲིན་པ་ Woj. chos kyi sPrin pa; Skt. dharmamegha.

birth

> Tib. སྐྱེ་བ་ Woj. sKye ba; Skt. jati. One of the twelve interdependent links of origination.

Bodhanath

> Bodhanath—or Bodha—is an area now subsumed within the city of Kathmandu. It is a place of pilgrimage because of the Great Chörten. *See:* chörten.

bodhisattva

> (Skt.) Tib. བྱང་ཆུབ་སེམས་དཔའ་ Woj. byang chub sems dPa'. A heroic being on the path to enlightenment.

Bodhisattvabuddhayana

> *See:* Sutrayana.

Bonfire Night

> Bonfire Night is a British tradition that occurs on the 5th of November every year, and includes the explosive display of fireworks and a bonfire. Ostensibly Bonfire Night 'celebrates' the successful defeat of the gunpowder plot in 1605 when Jesuits attempted to assassinate King James I and destroy parliament. This was in protest against the persecution of Roman Catholics. A guy—an effigy of Guy Fawkes, one of the conspirators—is often burned on the bonfire. I have always thought this a rather barbaric tradition, and certainly the burning of a guy never featured strongly in our family observance of Bonfire Night.

cause and effect

> Cause and effect is one view of karma (*see:* karma) that every action creates an effect, and there follows from this the concept that every negative action has to be eradicated through a corresponding positive action.

This can become a rather fatalistic and deterministic view and turns practitioners into accountants – attempting to resolve the karmic balance sheet on a daily basis. The Vajrayana view of karma is one of 'perception and response' rather than 'cause and effect'. *See:* perception and response.

cham

Tib. འཆམ་ Woj. 'cham. Ritual dance.

charnel ground

Tib. དུར་ཁྲོད་ Woj. dur khrod; Skt. smasana; burial site. Historically there were eight great charnel grounds: 1) Cool Grove: Tib. བསིལ་བ་ཚལ་ Woj. bSil ba tshal – in the east; 2) Perfected in Body: Tib. སྐུ་ལ་རྫོགས་ Woj. sKu la rDzogs – to the south; 3) Lotus Mound: Tib. པད་མ་བརྩེགས་ Woj. pad ma brTsegs – to the west; 4) Lanka Mound, Tib. ལན་ཀ་བརྩེགས་ Woj. lan ka brTsegs – to the north; 5) Spontaneously Accomplished Mound: Tib. ལྷུན་གྲུབ་བརྩེགས་ Woj. lhun grub brTsegs – to the south-east; 6) Display of Great Secret: Tib. གསང་ཆེན་རོལ་པ་ Woj. gSang chen rol pa – to the south-west; 7) Pervasive Great Joy: Tib. ཧེ་ཆེན་བརྡལ་བ་ Woj. he chen brDal ba – to the north-west; 8) World Mound: Tib. འཇིག་རྟེན་བརྩེགས་ Woj. 'jig rTen brTsegs – to the north-east.

chö ké

Tib. ཆོས་སྐད་ Woj. chos sKad. The language of Dharma for practitioners of Himalayan Buddhism. Commonly it is referred to as 'Tibetan' but is also used by other Buddhist countries with their own language, such as Bhutan.

Chögyam Trungpa Rinpoche

Tib. རིག་འཛིན་ཆེན་པོ་ཆོས་རྒྱམ་དྲུང་པ་རིན་པོ་ཆེ་ Woj. rig 'dzin chen po chos rGyam drung pa rin po che – the Great Vidyadhara, Holder of Nondual Awareness (1939–1987).

Chögyam Trungpa Rinpoche was one of the most outstanding Tibetan Vajrayana Masters to teach in the West. He was the realised master who, more than any other, changed the teaching of Buddhism for Western people – Buddhadharma became a living possibility within the fabric of Western life. The Shambhala Publishing House has published a great number of books taken from his seminars. The two books referred to in this work are: *Glimpses of Abidharma*, and *Transcending Madness*.

chörten

Tib. མཆོད་རྟེན་ Woj. mChod rTen; Skt. stupa. A dome-shaped monument housing relics of the Buddha or an accomplished master, or used for offerings. The shape is symbolic of the elements: cube of earth, sphere of water, cone of fire, half moon of air, plus the circular shape indicated by the half moon represents space.

circumambulation

Tib. སྐོར་ར་ Woj. sKor ra. The action of moving around a sacred object or building – such as the circumambulation of the Great Chörten in Bodhanath. Pilgrims may just walk reciting mantra, or engage in prostrations as they walk.

compassion

Tib. སྙིང་རྗེ་ Woj. sNying je; Skt. karuna. One of the four immeasurables. The wish for all beings to be happy and free of suffering, and the willingness to engage in activity to bring this about.

consciousness

Tib. རྣམ་པར་ཤེས་པ་ Woj. rNam par shes pa; Skt. vijnana. One of the twelve interdependent links of origination.

contact

Tib. རེག་པ་ Woj. reg pa; Skt. sparsa. One of the twelve interdependent links of origination.

craving

Tib. སྲེད་པ་ Woj. sred pa; Skt. trsna. One of the twelve interdependent links of origination.

cyclic existence

Tib. སྲིད་པ་འཁོར་བ་ Woj. srid pa 'khor ba; Skt. samsara. The teachings revealed by the Wheel of Life imagery. All beings cycle continually through birth, old age, sickness and death, seeking satisfaction and failing to find it.

dam-chan

See: protector.

death

Tib. རྒ་ཤི་ Woj. rGa shi; Skt. jara-marana. Also encompasses sickness and old age. One of the twelve interdependent links of origination.

demi-god or jealous god realm being

Tib. ལྷ་མ་ཡིན་ Woj. lha ma yin; Skt. asura – literally 'not god'.

Dharma

(Skt.) Tib. ཆོས་ Woj. chos. The true nature of everything – as it is. The word is used to refer to the teachings of Buddhism which describe the nature of reality.

dissatisfaction

Tib. སྡུག་བསྔལ་ Woj. sdDug bsNgal; Skt. dhukkha. Usually translated as 'suffering', dissatisfaction is a range: experience differing slightly from what is wished, to abject pain and misery.

dorje tsig dun

Tib. རྡོ་རྗེ་ཚིག་བདུན་ Woj. rDo rJe tshig bDun – the seven line prayer of Guru Rinpoche, or the seven thunderbolt phrases.

dualism

Buddhism teaches that reality is the nonduality of emptiness and form. Emptiness is the empty potential from which form arises. Form is the multivarious manifestations that arise, each unique and individuated. Form continually arises and dissolves, changes and moves. When emptiness and form are regarded as separate, this is called 'dualism'. When one is desired and the other rejected, beings experience dissatisfaction. For example if meeting someone is wished for, but the meeting is cancelled, that emptiness causes unhappiness. Alternatively, if you do not wish to meet someone you find unpleasant, and then end up sitting next to them in a meeting, the form of that situation causes unhappiness.

Dzogchen

(Tib.) རྫོགས་ཆེན་ Woj. rDzogs chen; Skt. atiyoga. In the nine vehicle system of the Nyingma Tradition, there are three vehicles of Sutrayana, and six vehicles of Vajrayana – three Outer Tantras and Three Inner Tantras. When the third of the Inner Tantras—Ati yoga—is regarded as a separate vehicle, it is commonly referred to by the Tibetan word *Dzogchen*. The base, path, and result of Dzogchen are all nonduality.

eight worldly dharmas

Tib. འཇིག་རྟེན་གྱི་ཆོས་བརྒྱད་ Woj. 'jig rTen gyi chos brGyad. Although these are enumerated as the *eight* worldly dharmas, different traditions have varying sets of eight, so in fact twelve can be enumerated.

In the Aro gTér Lineage the set of eight are: 1 & 2. gain and loss: Tib. རྙེད་པ་ / མ་རྙེད་པ་ Woj. rNyed pa / ma rNyed pa; 3 & 4. hope and fear: Tib. རེ་དོགས་གཉིས་ Woj. re dogs gNyis; 5 & 6. meeting and parting: Tib. འདུས་པའ་བྲལ་བ་ Woj. 'dus pa' bral ba; 7 & 8: praise and blame, Tib. བསྟོད་པ་ / སྨད་པ་ Woj. bsTod pa / sMad pa. Two more sets that can also be found are: pleasure and pain: Tib. བདེ་བ་ / སྡུག་ བསྔལ་ Woj. bDe ba / sDug bsNgal; and, fame and shame: Tib. སྙན་ གྲགས་ / ངོ་ཚ་ Woj. sNyan grags / ngo tsha.

emptiness

Tib. སྟོང་པ་ཉིད་ Woj. sTong pa nyid; Skt. shunyata. The empty potential from which form arises. Emptiness has the qualities of permanence, continuity and of being unchanging.

equanimity

Tib. བཏང་སྙོམས་ Woj. bTang sNyoms; Skt. upeksha. One of the four immeasurables. To regard the needs of others as important as one's own needs. To regard helping all beings as an equal responsibility; impartially, irrespective of who they are and one's relationship with them.

error

Tib. སྡིག་པ་ Woj. sDig pa.

five elements

The five elements are the 'building blocks' of reality – the basis of everyone and everything, everywhere. 1. Earth: Tib. ས་ Woj. sa; 2. water: Tib. ཆུ་ Woj. chu; 3. fire: Tib. མེ་ Woj. me; 4. air: Tib. རླུང་ Woj. rLung; and 5. space: Tib. ཀློང་ Woj. kLong.

form

Tib. གཟུགས་ Woj. gZugs; Skt. rupa. That which arises from emptiness. Form has the qualities of impermanence, always changing, and moving.

formations

Mental formations. Tib. འདུ་བྱེད་ Woj. 'du byed; Skt. samskara. One of the twelve interdependent links of origination.

go-kar-chang-lo

Tib. གོས་དཀར་ལྕང་ལོ་ Woj. gos dKar lCang lo – literally 'white clothes, long hair'. This term refers to the non-monastic, non-celibate yogic practitioners.

god realm being

Tib. ལྷ་ Woj. lha; Skt. deva.

gradual path

It is said that Shakyamuni Buddha referred to his path of practice as 'gradual training'. Wikipedia offers the following quotation: *Just as the ocean has a gradual shelf, a gradual slope, a gradual inclination, with a sudden drop-off only after a long stretch, in the same way this discipline of Dhamma has a gradual training, a gradual performance, a gradual progression, with a penetration to gnosis only after a long stretch. (Udana, 5.5)*

grasping

Tib. ལེན་པ་ Woj. len pa; Skt. upadana. One of the twelve interdependent links of origination.

guardians of the four directions

Tib. ཆོས་སྐྱོང་ Woj. chos sKyong; Skt. dikpala. The four guardians are: 1. Tib. ཛཾ་བྷ་ལ་ Woj. dzam bha la or Tib. རྨུགས་འཛིན་ Woj. rMugs 'dzin; Skt. Kubera – in the North; 2. Tib. གཤིན་རྗེ་ཆོས་རྒྱལ་ Woj. gShin rJe chos rGyal; Skt. Yama – in the South; 3. Tib. དབང་པོ་ Woj. dBang po; Skt. Indra – in the East; 4. Tib. ནུབ་ཀྱི་ཕྱོགས་སྐྱོང་ Woj. nub kyi phyogs sKyong; Skt. Varuna – in the West.

Guru Rinpoche

The Lotus-born Lama and Tantric Buddha. The founder of Buddhism in the Himalayan Buddhist countries in the 8th and 9th centuries. Ngak'chang Rinpoche says of him: *He is utterly unprecedented in every sense in terms of compassion, wisdom, and power. He opened the door to realisation to innumerable beings and provided systems of methodology so vividly variegated and indefinitely unfolding as to provide the means of liberation of every style of dualistic bewilderment throughout the ages. His inspiration is as potent now as it ever has been and the lineages he inspired continue today, to provide the spiritual nourishment for accomplishment in every sphere of Dharma.*

heart sutra

Tib. ཉིང་ཐིག་མདོ་ Woj. nying thig mDo; Skt. prajnaparamita sutra. The Heart Sutra establishes the principle of nonduality: *form is emptiness; emptiness is form.*

hell realm being

Tib. དམྱལ་བ་ Woj. dMyal ba; Skt. naraka.

Himalayan Buddhism

When Buddhism first came to the West from the Himalayan region, the term 'Tibetan Buddhism' was used to describe it. This is not an accurate term, however, as the Buddhism of Bhutan, for example, is as rich and extensive as the Buddhism that developed in Tibet. The term 'Himalayan Buddhism' encompasses all forms of Buddhism that exist in that region. In Tibet, the Gélug School was founded in the 14th century and had become dominant by the 20th century. This is an entirely monastic tradition. The Gélug School did not become dominant in Bhutan, so the form of Buddhism found there is more in keeping with the Vajrayana established by Guru Rinpoche in the 8th and 9th centuries.

human realm being

Tib. མི་ Woj. mi; Skt. manusa.

hungry ghost realm being

Tib. ཡི་དྭགས་ Woj. yi dwags / yi dvags; Skt. preta.

ignorance

Tib. མ་རིག་པ་ Woj. ma rig pa; Skt. avidya. One of the twelve interdependent links of origination.

illusory self

See: self-existing 'I'.

immeasurables, four

Tib. ཚད་མེད་བཞི་ Woj. tshad med bZhi; Skt. catvary-apramanani. The four unbounded states: 1. loving kindness: Tib. བྱམས་པ་ Woj. byams pa; Skt. maitri metta bhavana; 2. compassion: Tib. སྙིང་རྗེ་ Woj. sNying je; Skt. karuna; 3. empathetic joy: Tib. དགའ་བ་ Woj. dGa' ba; Skt. mudita; 4. equanimity: Tib. བཏང་སྙོམས་ Woj. bTang sNyoms; Skt. upeksha. The practise of these four awakens the mind to full realisation.

impermanence and death

Tib. མི་རྟག་པ་དང་འཆི་བ་ Woj. mi rTag pa dang 'chi ba; Skt. anitya marana.

indifference

Tib. མ་རིག་པ་ Woj. ma rig pa; Skt. moha. *See:* root misconceptions.

Inner Tantras, three

Tib. ནང་རྒྱུད་སྡེ་གསུམ་ Woj. nang rGyud sDe gSum; Skt. abhya tantra.
1. Tib. རྣལ་འབྱོར་ཆེན་པོ་ Woj. rNal 'byor chen po; Skt. mahayoga tantra;
2. Tib. རྗེས་སུ་རྣལ་འབྱོར་ Woj. rJes su rNal 'byor; Skt. anuyoga tantra;
3. Tib. རྫོགས་ཆེན་ rDzogs chen; Skt. atiyoga tantra.

joy, empathetic

Tib. དགའ་བ་ Woj. dGa' ba; Skt. mudita. One of the four immeasurables. The capacity to experience joy from others' happiness, good luck, success and well-being as if it were your own.

karma

(Skt.) Tib. ལས་ Woj. las. The patterning created in the mindstream through perception and response. To create a complete pattern there must be three factors: 1. intention; 2. engaging in the activity of the intention; 3. satisfaction of having engaged in the intended activity. Perception gives rise to intention, and response acts on that intention.

Kathmandu

Capital city of Nepal in the Himalayan region.

Khandro Déchen

Khandro Déchen Tsédrup Rolpa'i Yeshé, Tib. མཁའ་འགྲོ་བདེ་ཆེན་ཚེ་གྲུབ་རོལ་པའི་ཡེ་ཤེས་ Woj. mKha' 'gro bDe chen tshe grub rol pa'i ye shes (b. 1960) is the spiritual partner and wife of Ngak'chang Rinpoche; Lineage Holder of the Aro gTér. Khandro Déchen is the incarnation or Jomo A-yé Khandro (Woj. jo mo A ye mKha' 'gro) – as recognised by Kyabjé Künzang Dorje Rinpoche (Woj.sKyabs rJe kun bZang rDo rJe) and Jomo Sam'phel Déchen Rinpoche (Woj. jo mo bSam 'phel bDe chen rin po che).

kindness

See: loving kindness.

knowing

Tib. ཡེ་ཤེས་ Woj. ye shes; Skt. jnana. Wisdom Mind, Primordial Wisdom – the capacity to *know* without need of study or intellectual understanding.

Lama Mani

Teaching through story telling; *see:* Lama Mani https://dharma-documentaries.net/lama-mani-tibetan-storytelling

lhakhang

Tib. ལྷ་ཁང་ Woj. lha khang; Skt. devakula. Temple, chapel, shrine, shrine room. A place where objects to support religious practice are housed – such as statues and thangkas, and where meditation and other practices are practised.

liberation

Tib. གྲོལ་ Woj. grol; Skt. moksha.

links of interdependent origination, twelve

Tib. རྟེན་འབྲེལ་བཅུ་གཉིས་ Woj. rTen 'brel bCu gNyis; Skt. nidanas. The twelve links that create cyclic existence. Each is a cause for the following link.

longevity, symbols of, six

Tib. ཚེ་རིང་རྣམ་དྲུག Woj. tshe ring rNam drug. 1. rockface or cliff: Tib. བྲག་ཚེ་རིང་ Woj. brag tshe ring; 2. water: Tib. ཆུ་ཚེ་རིང་ Woj. chu tshe ring; 3. tree/wood: Tib. ཤིང་ཚེ་རིང་ Woj. shing tshe ring; 4. human long life: Tib. མི་ཚེ་རིང་ Woj. mi tshe ring; 5. white crane: Tib. བྱ་ཚེ་རིང་ Woj. bya tshe ring; 6. deer: Tib. རི་དྭགས་ཚེ་རིང་ Woj. ri dwags tshe ring. These are depicted as an elderly person sitting beneath a tree in front of a cliff face, with deer and white crane. Water may be in the form of a waterfall coming from the cliff, or a lake, or the elderly person may be pouring water from a vessel. This image is common on the outer walls of lhakhangs in Bhutan, in my experience, but I have not seen it so often in Nepal.

loving kindness

Tib. བྱམས་པ་ Woj. byams pa; Skt. maitri metta bhavana. One of the four immeasurables. Selfless, open-hearted warmth toward others.

Lord of Death

See: Yama.

Maitreya

(Skt.) Tib. བྱམས་པ་ Woj. byams pa. In the Rice Seedling Sutra, the conversation about the twelve interdependent links of causation takes place between Bodhisattva Maitreya and the Venerable Sariputra. Maitreya is prophecised as the future Buddha and is said to currently be residing in Tushita Heaven.

mandala

(Skt.) Tib. དཀྱིལ་འཁོར་ Woj. dKyil 'khor. Literally *centre and periphery*. A mandala is a symbolic geometric representation of the sphere of the visionary being used in visualisation practices. A mandala offering set consists of a base, rings, and a top piece. There are usually three rings, but there can be more. The mandala can be made of metal or wood. A practitioner offers the entire phenomenal universe using this symbolic device. A ritual practice is intoned whilst doing this. First the base is symbolically cleaned and the largest ring placed upon it. This is filled with rice, beads, or precious stones until full. Then the next ring is put on top and filled, and so on for the third ring. Finally the top piece is placed and then the full mandala is tipped forward away from the practitioner as an offering. The process is then repeated. For preliminary practice this will be completed 100,000 times.

manifestations, eight

Guru Rinpoche, the Tantric Buddha, is depicted as having displayed eight manifestations.
1. Tib. པད་མ་རྒྱལ་པོ་ Woj. pad ma rGyal po; Skt. Padmaraja – the Lotus Prince; 2. Tib. རྡོ་རྗེ་འཆང་ Woj. rDo rJe 'chang; Skt. Vajradhara – the Vajra-holder; 3. Tib. ཉི་མ་འོད་གཟེར་ Woj. nyi ma 'od gZer; Skt. Suryabhasa – Rays of the Sun;

4. Tib. ༄༅་ཤེང་གི་ Woj. sha kya seng ge; Skt. Sakyasimha – Lion of the Shakya clan; 5. Tib. སེང་གི་སྒྲ་སྒྲོག་ Woj. seng ge sGra sGrog; Skt. Simhanada – the Lion-voiced; 6. Tib. པད་མ་འབྱུང་གནས་ Woj. pad ma 'byung gNas; Skt. Padmasambhava – the Lotus-born; 7. Tib. བློ་ལྡན་མཆོག་སྲེད་ Woj. bLo lDan mChog sred; Skt. Mativat Vararuci – the Emperor; 8. Tib. རྡོ་རྗེ་གྲོ་ལོད་ Woj. rDo rJe gro lod; Skt. Guru Vajra – Wisdom-chaos.

mantra recitation

Mantras are phrases composed of sacred syllables that evoke the qualities of an awareness-being. The recitation of mantra is a major practice of Vajrayana Buddhism.

Memorial Chörten

The Memorial Chörten in Thimphu, Bhutan, was built in 1974 to honour the third Druk Gyalpo, Jigme Dorji Wangchuck (1928–1972). It was consecrated by Düd'jom Rinpoche, Jigdrel Yeshé Dorje.

merit

Tib. བསོད་ནམས་ Woj. bSod nams; Skt: puṇya. Sometimes known as 'white karma', merit is the accomplishment of intention and action that leads toward realisation and liberation from cyclic existence.

method

Tib. ཐབས་ Woj. thabs; Skt. upaya. Skilful means. The practices employed to bring about awakening.

monk

Tib. དགེ་སློང་ Woj. dGe sLong; Skt. bhiksu. A fully ordained male monastic practitioner.

morality

Tib. ཚུལ་ཁྲིམས་ Woj. tshul khrims; Skt. shila. Also translates as 'discipline' or 'ethics'. One of the ten perfections, *see:* perfections, ten.

Mordor

The realm of the evil Sauron in JRR Tolkein's *Lord of the Rings* trilogy.

naljorma/pa

Tib. རྣལ་འབྱོར་མ་/ པ་ Woj. rNal 'byor ma/pa; Skt. yogini/yogi, . A practitioner of the non-celibate, gos dKar lCang lo'i sDe, *see:* go-kar-chang-lo.

naljors, four

Tib. རྣལ་འབྱོར་བཞི་ Woj. rNal 'byor bZhi; Skt. yoga. The four naljors are the preliminary practices of Dzogchen: 1. Tib. ཞི་གནས་ Woj. zhi gNas; Skt. samatha – calm abiding; 2. Tib. ལྷག་མཐོང་ Woj. lhag mThong; Skt. Vipassana – further vision; 3. Tib. གཉིས་མེད་ Woj. gNyis med; Skt. advaya – not two, nonduality; 4. Tib. ལྷུན་གྲུབ་ Woj. lhun grub; Skt. anabhoga – spontaneity.

name and form

Tib. མིང་དང་གཟུགས་ Woj. ming dang gZugs; Skt. nama-rupa. One of the twelve interdependent links of origination.

nature of Mind, natural state of Mind

Tib. ཆོས་ཉིད་ Woj. chos nyid; Skt. dharmata.

Ngak'chang Rinpoche

Tib. སྔགས་འཆང་རིན་པོ་ཆེ་ Woj. sNgags 'chang rin po che. Lineage Holder of the Aro gTér. He is the Aro tulku, incarnation of Aro Yeshé (Woj. A ro ye shes) who was the son of A ro Lingma (Woj. a ro gLing ma), as recognised by Kyabjé Düd'jom Rinpoche Jig'drèl Yeshé Dorje (Woj. bDud 'joms 'jigs bral ye shes rDo rJe rin po che).

ngakma/pa

Tib. སྔགས་མ་ / པ་ Woj. sNgags ma/pa; Skt. mantrini/mantrin. Literally mantra woman/man. A practitioner of the non-celibate, gos dKar lCang lo'i sDe, *see:* go-kar-chang-lo.

noble truths, four

Tib. འཕགས་པའི་བདེན་པ་བཞི་ Woj. 'phags pa'i bDen pa bZhi; Skt. catvaryaryasatyani. The first turning of the wheel of Dharma. 1. The truth of dissatisfaction: Tib. སྡུག་བསྔལ་བདེན་པ་ Woj. sDug bsNgal bDen pa; Skt. dukkha-satyam; 2. The truth of the cause of dissatisfaction: Tib. ཀུན་འབྱུང་བའི་བདེན་པ་ Woj. kun 'byung ba'i bDen pa; Skt. samudaya-satya; 3. The truth of the cessation of dissatisfaction: Tib. འགོག་པའི་བདེན་པ་ Woj. 'gog pa'i bDen pa; Skt. nirodha-satya; 4. The truth of the path that leads to the cessation of dissatisfaction: Tib. ལམ་གྱི་བདེན་པ་ Woj. lam gyi bDen pa; Skt. marga-satya.

nonduality

See: rigpa.

nun

Tib. དགེ་སློང་མ་ Woj. dGe sLong ma; Skt. bhiksuni. A female monastic practitioner.

Nyingma

Tib. སྔ་འགྱུར་རྙིང་མ་ Woj. sNga 'gyur rNying ma. The most ancient form of Himalayan Buddhism founded by Guru Rinpoche in the 8th century. The Nyingma Tradition is commonly referred to as one of the four schools of Buddhism: Nyingma, Sakya (Tib. ས་སྐྱ་ Woj. sa sKya), Kagyu (Tib. བཀའ་བརྒྱུད་ Woj. bKa' brGyud), and Gélug (Tib. དགེ་ལུགས་ Woj. dGe lugs).

original sin

In Christian doctrine human beings are considered to be born in a state of sin, through being born from a woman's womb. This refers back to the story in the book of Genesis, where Adam and Eve are expulsed from the garden of Eden, which meant that all their offspring were conceived in sin.

Outer Tantras, three

Tib. ཕྱི་རྒྱུད་སྡེ་གསུམ་ Woj. phyi rGyud sDe gSum; Skt. bahya tantra:
1. Tib. བྱ་བ་ Woj. bya ba; Skt. kriya;
2. Tib. སྤྱོད་པ་ Woj. sPyod pa; Skt. upa or carya; and
3. Tib. རྣལ་འབྱོར་ Woj. rNal 'byor; Skt. yoga.

paramitas, ten

See: perfections, ten.

pecha

Tib. དཔེ་ཆ་ Woj. dPe cha. A Tibetan loose-leaf book. They often have top and bottom covers made of wood or another stiff material, and may be wrapped in cloth to protect them. The pages of such books are wide and short, having traditionally been printed using carved woodblocks.

perception and response

Perception and response create karmic patterning. Once perceived, phenomena are judged and classified as either attractive, unattractive or neutral. From this, intention arises and then response. In this view, the patterning of karma exists in the present moment alone. If perception is direct and response appropriate and based in wisdom and kindness—rather than in delusion—this is a moment of awakening. If moment by moment experience becomes awakened in this way, the patterns of negative karma simply disappear – they do not have to be unravelled action by action.

perfections, ten

Tib. ཕ་རོལ་ཏུ་ཕྱིན་པ་དྲུག་ཕར་བཅུ་ Woj. pha rol tu phyin pa drug phar bCu; Skt. paramita. 1. generosity: Tib. སྦྱིན་པ་ Woj. sByin pa; Skt. dana; 2. discipline: Tib. ཚུལ་ཁྲིམས་ Woj. tshul khrims; Skt. shila; 3. patience: Tib. བཟོད་པ་ Woj. bZod pa; Skt. kshanti; 4. diligence: Tib. བརྩོན་འགྲུས་ Woj. brTson 'grus; Skt. virya; 5. openness, concentration: Tib. བསམ་གཏན་ Woj. bSam gTen; Skt. dhyana; 6. knowledge: Tib. ཤེས་རབ་ Woj. shes rab; Skt. prajna; 7. method: Tib. ཐབས་ Woj. thabs; Skt. upaya; 8. aspiration: Tib. སྨོན་ལམ་ Woj. sMon lam; Skt. pranidhana; 9. strength, power: Tib. སྟོབས་ Woj. sTobs; Skt. bala; 10. primordial wisdom: Tib. ཡེ་ཤེས་ Woj. ye shes; Skt. jnana.

Pratyekabuddhayana

See: Sutrayana.

prayer wheel

Tib. ཆོས་འཁོར་ Woj. chos 'khor. A cylinder with a central spindle that allows the cylinder to spin freely. The size of prayer wheels can vary from small hand-held devices, to several metres high. Inside the cylinder are rolls of mantra.

Spinning the prayer wheel is considered to be the equivalent of intoning the mantras within it, and also mirrors 'turning the wheel of Dharma'. The hand-held prayer wheels have a weighted cord or chain that aids momentum as it spins.

Precious Human rebirth

Tib. མི་ལུས་རིན་ཆེན་ Woj. mi lus rin chen. In order to elevate a human rebirth to the status of a Precious Human rebirth, it is necessary to have certain qualities and embrace certain opportunities: 1. being born in a *time* where Buddhist teaching exists; 2. being born in a *place* where Buddhist teaching exists; 3. having the capacity to understand the consequences of positive and negative actions; 4. having the capacity to hear and understand basic Buddhist teachings; 5. to be free of physical and mental problems that prevent one from hearing and understanding Dharma; 6. to be free of gross suffering, such as starvation, pain, serious illness, etc.; 7. to be born in a place where there are no obstructions to hearing Dharma, such as war, prejudice; 8. to have an interest in Buddhist teachings. This is not a definitive list as the teachings on the Precious Human rebirth can be extensive.

professional practitioners

Practitioners who have taken vows and live within the context of those vows and their practice. In the monastic traditions these will be nuns and monks. In the gö kar chang lo'i dé these will be ngakmas and ngakpas, naljormas and naljorpas.

prostration

Tib. ཕྱག་འཚལ་བ་ Woj. phyag 'tsal ba. Prostrations are commonly included in Buddhist practice. With a full prostration, the practioner prostrates their entire body flat on the floor. With a half prostration, the practitioner goes down to a kneeling position, touching the head to the floor. The preliminary practices for Vajrayana include an accumulation of 100,000 prostrations.

Pilgrims may circumambulate a sacred building or place by performing prostrations. The practitioner prostrates and places a marker, such as a pebble, where their hands extend in the full prostration. They then stand up, walk up to the place of the pebble, pick it up, and prostrate from that spot, once again placing the marker where their hands extend. At places of pilgrimage and practice, such as around the Great Chörten in Bodhanath, Kathmandu, you can find prostration boards. These are about 2 metres long and provide a clean and polished surface for the person practising prostrations.

protector

Tib. དམ་ཅན Woj. dam chan. Beings that have been oath bound to protect the Buddhist teachings and practitioners.

realisation

Another term for awakening or enlightenment. The union of wisdom and method, nonduality.

realms, six

Tib. རིགས་དྲུག Woj. rigs drug; Skt. loka – the realms of hell beings, hungry ghosts, animals, humane beings, demi-gods, and gods.

Rebirth

A Tibetan board game played with dice that teaches the basic principles of Buddhism. It was created in the 12th century and is possibly the source of the game 'Snakes and Ladders'. The book that accompanied my copy of the game has a lot of useful information about the realms and the paths of Buddhist practice: 'Rebirth – the Tibetan Game of Liberation', by Mark Tatz and Jody Kent, published by Rider and Company, 1977.

referentiality

> The process of filtering all experience through past experience, present prejudice and judgement, and/or future projection. Rather than perceiving directly, mental projections create a network of referentiality so that it becomes impossible to understand reality as it actually is.

renunciation

> Giving up ordinary life in favour of a spiritual life, in order to avoid the negative patterning created through desire and attraction, and hatred and aversion. Sutrayana is a path of renunciation and its ultimate expression is monasticism.

Rice Seedling Sutra

> Tib. སཱ་ལུའི་ལྗང་པ་ Woj. sa' (sA) lu'i lJang pa; Skt. salistamba. A teaching given by Shakyamuni Buddha to his monks on the twelve interdependent links of origination. It is presented as the Bodhisattva Maitreya explaining the teaching in response to a question by Sariputra. The quotes in this text are taken from a translation by the Dharmasagara Translation Group under the patronage and supervision of '84000: Translating the Words of the Buddha', 2018. The honorary patrons of 84000 include, His Majesty King Jigmé Khesar Namgyal Wangchuk and HRH Princess Kesang Wangmo Wangchuk of Bhutan. *See:* https://read.84000.co/translation/UT22084-062-010.html

rigpa

> Tib. རིག་པ་ Woj. rig pa; Skt. vidya. The wisdom of full awareness, full understanding, clarity, knowing, nondual realisation.

root misconceptions, three

Three poisons, or unwholesome roots. Tib. ཉོན་མོངས་པ་དུག་གསུམ་ Woj. nyon mongs pa dug gSum; Skt. trivisa. 1. ignorance or indifference: Tib. མ་རིག་པ་ Woj. ma rig pa; Skt. moha; 2. desire or attachment: Tib. འདོད་ཆགས་ Woj. 'dod chags; Skt. raga; 3. hatred or aversion: Tib. ཞེ་སྡང་ Woj. zhe sDang; Skt. dvesa. These three factors keep beings trapped in cyclic existence.

rosary

Tib. འཕྲེང་བ་ Woj. 'phreng ba; Skt. mala. Beads that are used like an abacus to record the number of mantras that have been recited.

sages, six

Tib. ཐུབ་པ་དྲུག་ Woj. thub pa drug; Skt. muni.
1. Hell realm Sage: Tib. ཆོས་ཀྱི་རྒྱལ་པོ་ Woj. chos kyi rGyal-po – King of Dharma; Skt. Yama Dharmaraja. He is black and holds a flame and a flask of water.
2. Hungry ghost realm Sage: Tib. ཁ་འབར་མ་ Woj. kha 'bar ma; Skt. Jvalamukha. This Sage is red, and holds a casket of treasures to overcome the miserliness, lack of appreciation and sense of impoverishment of the hungry ghost realm.
3. Animal realm Sage: Tib. སེང་གེ་རབ་བརྟན་ Woj. seng ge rab brTan; Skt. Sthirasimha – the Steadfast Lion. He is blue and holding a book to overcome the ignorance of the animal realm.
4. Human realm Sage: Tib. ཤཱཀྱ་སེང་གེ་ sha kya seng ge; Skt. Sakyamuni – Lion of the Shakya clan. He holds an alms bowl.
5. Jealous god realm Sage: Tib. ཐག་བཟང་རིས་ Woj. thag bZang ris; Skt. Vemacitra – Splendid Robe. This sage is usually shown holding armour and weaponry.
6. God realm Sage: Tib. བརྒྱ་བྱིན་ Woj. brGya byin; Indrasakra – Indra, the Lord of the Gods. This Sage holds a lute.

samsara

(Skt.) Tib. འཁོར་བ་ Woj. 'khor ba – cyclic existence; the continual cycle of birth, death, and rebirth.

Sariputra

(Skt.) (568–484 BCE) Tib. ཤཱ་རིའི་བུ་ Woj. sha ri'i bu. One of the closest disciples of Shakyamuni Buddha.

satisfaction

Tib. དགའ་བ་ Woj. dGa' ba. Happiness and joy.

self-existing 'I'

Tib. བདག་ Woj. bDag; Skt. atman. This is the fundamental misconception that somewhere within a being there exists a self, that is existent in some form, permanent, unchanging, continuous and has individuated definition. The existence of a 'soul' or self of this nature is denied in Buddhism. The experience of an 'I' is regarded as dream-like and illusory.

sensation

Tib. ཚོར་བ་ Woj. tshor ba; Skt. vedana. One of the twelve interdependent links of origination.

senses, six

Tib. སྐྱེ་མཆེད་དྲུག་ Woj. sKye mChed drug; Skt. sadayatana. One of the twelve interdependent links of origination.

Shakyamuni

The historic Buddha. Also known as Siddhartha Gautama. Accurate dates for his birth and death are unclear, but he lived and taught sometime between the 6th and 4th century BCE.

Shravakabuddhayana

See: Sutrayana.

shi-nè

> *See:* naljors, four.

shrineroom

> *See:* lhakhang.

silent sitting

> An expression to describe meditation that does not involve chanting, song or mantra recitation. *See:* naljors, four.

sin

> The concept of sin, or evil conduct is not usual in Buddhism, so this term translates more closely as 'error', or 'unskillful action'. *See:* error.

skandhas, five

> Tib. ཕུང་པོ་ལྔ་ Woj. phung po lNga; Skt. pancha skandha.
> 1. Form: Tib. གཟུགས་ Woj. gZugs; Skt. rupa; 2. feeling, sensation: Tib. ཚོར་བ་ Woj. tshor ba; Skt. vedana; 3. perception, discrimination: Tib. འདུ་ཤེས་ Woj. 'du shes; Skt. samjna; 4. intellect, mental formations: Tib. འདུ་བྱེད་ Woj. 'du byed; Skt. samskara; 5. consciousness, cognition: Tib. རྣམ་པར་ཤེས་པ་ Woj. rNam par shes pa; Skt. vijnana.

spheres of being, three

> Tib. སྐུ་གསུམ་ Woj. sKu gSum; Skt. kaya. 1. Tib. ཆོས་སྐུ་ Woj. chos sKu; Skt. dharmakaya; 2. Tib. ལོངས་སྐུ་ Woj. longs sKu; Skt. sambhogakaya; 3. Tib. སྤྲུལ་སྐུ་ Woj. sPrul sKu; Skt. nirmanakaya. Dharmakaya is the sphere of emptiness, unconditioned potentiality; sambhogakaya is the sphere of energy, intangible appearance; and nirmanakaya is the sphere of form, realised manifestation.

spiritual friend

Tib. དགེ་བའི་བཤེས་གཉེན་ Woj. dGe ba'i bShes gNyen; Skt. kalyanamitra. The spiritual friend is the teacher who imparts the teachings of Sutrayana which are generally applicable for all students.

spiritual materialism

This term was coined by Chögyam Trungpa Rinpoche – see *Cutting Through Spiritual Materialism*, Shambhala Publications. It refers to using the practices of Dharma as a means of making samsara more comfortable, or for status, or as things to collect, or as excuses for unkind behaviour, or as self-improvement techniques – rather than for liberation and benefitting all beings.

stages of progression, ten

The ten stages through which a Bodhisattva passes before gaining full enlightenment. *See:* bhumi, ten.

Star Trek

An American science-fiction television franchise created by Gene Roddenberry, and first aired on NBC in 1966. This ran for three seasons. In 1987 it was brought back as *Star Trek: the Next Generation*. Several films were made with the characters of this series, and the scene mentioned in this book comes from *Generations*, 1994. Ngakma Nor'dzin and Ngakpa 'ö-Dzin have always been interested in Science Fiction. It was some of the ideas about the nature of reality, presented in the Science Fiction literature of the 1950s and '60s, that led Ngakma Nor'dzin to the exploration of Dharma.

Sutra

(Skt.) Tib. མདོ་ Woj. mDo. The teachings of Shakyamuni Buddha.

Sutrayana

(Skt.) Tib. མདོའི་ཐེག་པ་ Woj. mDo'i theg pa. A term used when discussing the vehicles of Buddhism with regard to the nine-vehicle system of the Nyingma School. Sutrayana in this case includes the three vehicles of Sutrayana: 1. Tib. ཉན་ཐོས་ཀྱི་ཐེག་པ་ Woj. nyan thos kyi theg pa; Skt. shravakabuddhayana – the hearers; 2. Tib. རང་རྒྱལ་བའི་ཐེག་པ་ Woj. rang rGyal ba'i theg pa; Skt. pratyekabuddhayana – the solitary realisers; and 3. Tib. བྱང་ཆུབ་སེམས་དཔའི་ཐེག་པ་ Woj. byang chub sems dPa'i theg pa; Skt. bodhisattvabuddhayana – those who teach to benefit others.

Tantra

(Skt.), Tib. རྒྱུད་ Woj. rGyud. The path of transformation. *See:* Outer Tantra, Inner Tantra.

teacher

Tib. བླ་མ་ Woj. bLa ma; Skt. guru.

temple

See: lhakhang.

thangka

Tib. ཐང་ཀ་ Woj. thang ka. A painting on cloth.

thangka frame

Traditionally thangkas are mounted in a brocade frame. The various parts of the frame each have a symbolic meaning. As well as framing the image, there are covers to protect the thangka when being transported, or to hide it from view. The image painted in the thangka might be a secret visionary practice that can only be viewed by a practitioner who has received the appropriate transmission and preparation. The frame also has 'wings' – flat cloth ribbons that can be used to secure the thangka if it is rolled up, or to attach it to a tent when displayed.

Thimphu

The largest city in Bhutan, which became the capital in 1955.

tshogs'khorlo

The Vajra Feast: Tib. ཚོགས་ཀྱི་འཁོར་ལོ་ Woj. tshogs kyi 'khor lo; Skt ganachakra. A Vajrayana practice that involves sharing food. It is an opportunity to repair vow breakage, and to view all beings as realised. It is traditionally practised on the 10th and 25th days of the lunar month.

vajra master

Tib. རྡོ་རྗེ་སློབ་དཔོན་ Woj. rDo rJe sLob dPon; Skt. Vajracharya. In Vajrayana the relationship with the teacher is an essential aspect of the path. Vajrayana uses symbolic method and the teacher is needed to provide transmission of the method. The student engages with the presence, personality, and life circumstances of the teacher as a method of practice.

vajra melody

Tib. རྡོ་རྗེ་དབྱངས་ Woj. rDo rJe dbYangs. The melodies of mantras and prayers of inspiration. Oft times the melodies are engaged as a method of realisation by entering the dimension of the melody itself and the experience of singing.

Vajrayana

(Skt.) Tib. རྡོ་རྗེ་ཐེག་པ་ Woj. rDo rJe theg pa. The diamond or thunderbolt vehicle. Vajrayana is a blanket term that includes all the tantric vehicles. *See:* Outer Tantra, Inner Tantra.

vehicle

Tib. ཐེག་པ་ Woj. theg pa; Skt. yana. Different schools organise bodies of teachings according to their base, path, and result.

These are called vehicles because they transport the practitioner from delusion to realisation along a path consisting of methods of practice. The number and designation of vehicles varies from school to school.

vehicles, nine

Tib. ཐེག་པ་དགུ་ Woj. theg pa dGu. The Nyingma School of Buddhism uses a nine vehicle structure: three vehicles of Sutrayana, three outer Tantras, and three Inner Tantras. *See:* Inner Tantra, Outer Tantra, Sutra, Sutrayana, Vajrayana.

Wheel of Life

Tib. སྲིད་པ་འཁོར་ལོ་ Woj. srid pa 'khor lo; Skt. bhavacakra.

Yama

Tib. གཤིན་རྗེ་ཆོས་རྒྱལ་ Woj. gShin rJe chos rGyal; Skt. Yama Dharmaraja. The Lord of Death.

Yeshé Tsogyel

Tib. ཡེ་ཤེས་མཚོ་རྒྱལ་ Woj. ye shes mTsho rGyal; Skt. Jnana Sagara. The female tantric Buddha, and consort of Guru Rinpoche.

Zorig

Zorig Thangka Gallery – a thangka artists' co-operative based in Bodha, Kathmandu. This gallery painted the Wheel of Life thangka referenced in this book. Because of the pandemic it took over two years to complete. Zorig means 'arts and crafts': Tib. བཟོ་རིག་ Woj. bZo rig.

www.ingramcontent.com/pod-product-compliance
Lightning Source LLC
Chambersburg PA
CBHW060529090426
42735CB00011B/2432